Eat Well Live Well

READER'S DIGEST

Beautiful Baking

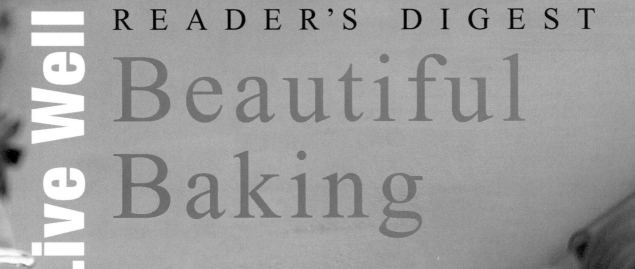

Eat Well Live Well

READER'S DIGEST
Beautiful Baking

Reader's
Digest

Published by The Reader's Digest Association Limited
London • New York • Sydney • Montreal

BEAUTIFUL BAKING is part of a series of cookery books called
EAT WELL LIVE WELL and was created by Amazon Publishing Limited.

Series Editor *Norma MacMillan*
Volume Editor *Jane Middleton*
Art Director *Ruth Prentice*
Photographic Direction *Ruth Prentice*
DTP *Peter Howard*
Editorial Assistant *Jasmine Brown*
Nutritionist *Fiona Hunter, BSc Hons (Nutri.), Dip. Dietetics*

CONTRIBUTORS
Writers *Catherine Atkinson, Anna Brandenburger, Linda Collister,*
Joanna Farrow, Christine France, Bridget Jones, Sara Lewis,
Angela Nilsen, Judith Wills
Recipe Testers *Catherine Atkinson, Maggie Pannell, Anne Sheasby, Gina Steer*
Photographers *Martin Brigdale, Gus Filgate, William Lingwood*
Stylist *Helen Trent*
Home Economists *Julie Beresford, Joanna Farrow, Bridget Sargeson,*
Linda Tubby, Sunil Vijayakar

FOR READER'S DIGEST
Project Editor *Rachel Warren Chadd*
Project Art Editor *Louise Turpin*
Production Controllers *Kathy Brown, Jane Holyer*

READER'S DIGEST GENERAL BOOKS
Editorial Director *Cortina Butler*
Art Director *Nick Clark*
Series Editor *Christine Noble*

ISBN 0 276 42476 X

First Edition Copyright © 2001
The Reader's Digest Association Limited
11 Westferry Circus, Canary Wharf, London E14 4HE
www.readersdigest.co.uk

Copyright © 2001 Reader's Digest Association Far East Limited
Philippines copyright © 2001 Reader's Digest Association Far East Limited

We are committed to both the quality of our products and the service we
provide to our customers. We value your comments, so please feel free to
contact us on 08705 113366, or by email at cust_service@readersdigest.co.uk
If you have any comments about the content of our books, you can contact us
at: gbeditorial@readersdigest.co.uk

Notes for the reader
• Use all metric or all imperial measures when preparing a recipe,
as the two sets of measurements are not exact equivalents.
• Recipes were tested using metric measures and conventional (not
fan-assisted) ovens. Medium eggs were used, unless otherwise
specified.
• Can sizes are approximate, as weights can vary slightly according
to the manufacturer.
• Preparation and cooking times are only intended as a guide.

The nutritional information in this book is for reference only.
The editors urge anyone with continuing medical problems or
symptoms to consult a doctor.

Contents

Eating well to live well

Eating a healthy diet can help you look good, feel great and have lots of energy. Nutrition fads come and go, but the simple keys to eating well remain the same: enjoy a variety of food – no single food contains all the vitamins, minerals, fibre and other essential components you need for health and vitality – and get the balance right by looking at the proportions of the different foods you eat. Add some regular exercise too – at least 30 minutes a day, 3 times a week – and you'll be helping yourself to live well and make the most of your true potential.

Getting it into proportion

Current guidelines are that most people in the UK should eat more starchy foods, more fruit and vegetables, and less fat, meat products and sugary foods. It is almost impossible to give exact amounts that you should eat, as every single person's requirements vary, depending on size, age and the amount of energy expended during the day. However, nutrition experts have suggested an ideal balance of the different foods that provide us with energy (calories) and the nutrients needed for health. The number of daily portions of each of the food groups will vary from person to person – for example, an active teenager might need to eat up to 14 portions of starchy carbohydrates every day, whereas a sedentary adult would only require 6 or 7 portions – but the proportions of the food groups in relation to each other should ideally stay the same.

More detailed explanations of food groups and nutritional terms can be found on pages 156–158, together with brief guidelines on amounts which can be used in conjunction with the nutritional analyses of the recipes. A simple way to get the balance right, however, is to imagine a daily 'plate' divided into the different food groups. On the imaginary 'plate', starchy carbohydrates fill at least one-third of the space, thus constituting the main part of your meals. Fruit and vegetables fill the same amount of space. The remaining third of the 'plate' is divided mainly between protein foods and dairy foods, with just a little space allowed for foods containing fat and sugar. These are the proportions to aim for.

It isn't essential to eat the ideal proportions on the 'plate' at every meal, or even every day – balancing them over a week or two is just as good. The healthiest diet for you and your family is one that is generally balanced and sustainable in the long term.

Our daily plate

Starchy carbohydrate foods: eat 6–14 portions a day

At least 50% of the calories in a healthy diet should come from carbohydrates, and most of that from starchy foods – bread, potatoes and other starchy vegetables, pasta, rice and cereals. For most people in the UK this means doubling current intake. Starchy carbohydrates are the best foods for energy. They also provide protein and essential vitamins and minerals, particularly those from the B group. Eat a variety of starchy foods, choosing wholemeal or wholegrain types whenever possible, because the fibre they contain helps to prevent constipation, bowel disease, heart disease and other health problems.

What is a portion of starchy foods?
Some examples are: 3 tbsp breakfast cereal • 2 tbsp muesli • 1 slice of bread or toast • 1 bread roll, bap or bun • 1 small pitta bread, naan bread or chapatti • 3 crackers or crispbreads • 1 medium-sized potato • 1 medium-sized plantain or small sweet potato • 2 heaped tbsp boiled rice • 2 heaped tbsp boiled pasta.

Fruit and vegetables: eat at least 5 portions a day

Nutrition experts are unanimous that we would all benefit from eating more fruit and vegetables each day – a total of at least 400 g (14 oz) of fruit and vegetables (edible part) is the target. Fruit and vegetables provide vitamin C for immunity and healing, and other 'antioxidant' vitamins and minerals for protection against cardiovascular disease and cancer. They also offer several 'phytochemicals' that help protect against cancer, and B vitamins, especially folate, which is important for women planning a pregnancy, to prevent birth defects. All of these, plus other nutrients, work together to boost well-being.

Antioxidant nutrients (e.g. vitamins C and beta-carotene, which are mainly derived from fruit and vegetables) and vitamin E help to prevent harmful free radicals in the body initiating or accelerating cancer, heart disease, cataracts, arthritis, general ageing, sun damage to skin, and damage to sperm. Free radicals occur naturally as a by-product of normal cell function, but are also caused by pollutants such as tobacco smoke and over-exposure to sunlight.

What is a portion of fruit or vegetables?
Some examples are: 1 medium-sized portion of vegetables or salad • 1 medium-sized piece of fresh fruit • 6 tbsp (about 140 g/5 oz) stewed or canned fruit • 1 small glass (100 ml/3½ fl oz) fruit juice.

Dairy foods: eat 2–3 portions a day

Dairy foods, such as milk, cheese, yogurt and fromage frais, are the best source of calcium for strong bones and teeth, and important for the nervous system. They also provide some protein for growth and repair, vitamin B_{12}, and vitamin A for healthy eyes. They are particularly valuable foods for young children, who need full-fat versions at least up to age 2. Dairy foods are also especially important for adolescent girls to prevent the development of osteoporosis later in life, and for women throughout life generally.

To limit fat intake, wherever possible adults should choose lower-fat dairy foods, such as semi-skimmed milk and low-fat yogurt.

What is a portion of dairy foods?
Some examples are: 1 medium-sized glass (200 ml/7 fl oz) milk • 1 matchbox-sized piece (40 g/1½ oz) Cheddar cheese • 1 small pot of yogurt • 125 g (4½ oz) cottage cheese or fromage frais.

Protein foods: eat 2–4 portions a day

Lean meat, fish, eggs and vegetarian alternatives provide protein for growth and cell repair, as well as iron to prevent anaemia. Meat also provides B vitamins for healthy nerves and digestion, especially vitamin B_{12}, and zinc for growth and healthy bones and skin. Only moderate amounts of these protein-rich foods are required. An adult woman needs about 45 g of protein a day and an adult man 55 g, which constitutes about 11% of a day's calories. This is less than the current average intake. For optimum health, we need to eat some protein every day.

What is a portion of protein-rich food?

Some examples are: 3 slices (85–100 g/3–3½ oz) of roast beef, pork, ham, lamb or chicken • about 100 g (3½ oz) grilled offal • 115–140 g (4–5 oz) cooked fillet of white or oily fish (not fried in batter) • 3 fish fingers • 2 eggs (up to 7 a week) • about 140 g/5 oz baked beans • 60 g (2¼ oz) nuts, peanut butter or other nut products.

Foods containing fat: 1–5 portions a day

Unlike fruit, vegetables and starchy carbohydrates, which can be eaten in abundance, fatty foods should not exceed 33% of the day's calories in a balanced diet, and only 10% of this should be from saturated fat. This quantity of fat may seem a lot, but it isn't – fat contains more than twice as many calories per gram as either carbohydrate or protein.

Overconsumption of fat is a major cause of weight and health problems. A healthy diet must contain a certain amount of fat to provide fat-soluble vitamins and essential fatty acids, needed for the development and function of the brain, eyes and nervous system, but we only need a small amount each day – just 25 g is required, which is much less than we consume in our Western diet. The current recommendations from the Department of Health are a maximum of 71 g fat (of this, 21.5 g saturated) for women each day and 93.5 g fat (28.5 g saturated) for men. The best sources of the essential fatty acids are natural fish oils and pure vegetable oils.

What is a portion of fatty foods?

Some examples are: 1 tsp butter or margarine • 2 tsp low-fat spread • 1 tsp cooking oil • 1 tbsp mayonnaise or vinaigrette (salad dressing) • 1 tbsp cream • 1 individual packet of crisps.

Foods containing sugar: 0–2 portions a day

Although many foods naturally contain sugars (e.g. fruit contains fructose, milk lactose), health experts recommend that we limit 'added' sugars. Added sugars, such as table sugar, provide only calories – they contain no vitamins, minerals or fibre to contribute to health, and it is not necessary to eat them at all. But, as the old adage goes, 'a little of what you fancy does you good' and sugar is no exception. Denial of foods, or using them as rewards or punishment, is not a healthy attitude to eating, and can lead to cravings, binges and yo-yo dieting. Sweet foods are a pleasurable part of a well-balanced diet, but added sugars should account for no more than 11% of the total daily carbohydrate intake.

In assessing how much sugar you consume, don't forget that it is a major ingredient of many processed and ready-prepared foods.

What is a portion of sugary foods?

Some examples are: 3 tsp sugar • 1 heaped tsp jam or honey • 2 biscuits • half a slice of cake • 1 doughnut • 1 Danish pastry • 1 small bar of chocolate • 1 small tube or bag of sweets.

Too salty

Salt (sodium chloride) is essential for a variety of body functions, but we tend to eat too much through consumption of salty processed foods, 'fast' foods and ready-prepared foods, and by adding salt in cooking and at the table. The end result can be rising blood pressure as we get older, which puts us at higher risk of heart disease and stroke. Eating more vegetables and fruit increases potassium intake, which can help to counteract the damaging effects of salt.

Alcohol in a healthy diet

In recent research, moderate drinking of alcohol has been linked with a reduced risk of heart disease and stroke among men and women over 45. However, because of other risks associated with alcohol, particularly in excessive quantities, no doctor would recommend taking up drinking if you are teetotal. The healthiest pattern of drinking is to enjoy small amounts of alcohol with food, to have alcohol-free days and always to avoid getting drunk. A well-balanced diet is vital because nutrients from food (vitamins and minerals) are needed to detoxify the alcohol.

Water – the best choice

Drinking plenty of non-alcoholic liquid each day is an often overlooked part of a well-balanced diet. A minimum of 8 glasses (which is about 2 litres/3½ pints) is the ideal. If possible, these should not all be tea or coffee, as these are stimulants and diuretics, which cause the body to lose liquids, taking with them water-soluble vitamins. Water is the best choice. Other good choices are fruit or herb teas or tisanes, fruit juices – diluted with water, if preferred – or semi-skimmed milk (full-fat milk for very young children). Fizzy sugary or acidic drinks such as cola are more likely to damage tooth enamel than other drinks.

As a guide to the vitamin and mineral content of foods and recipes in the book, we have used the following terms and symbols, based on the percentage of the daily RNI provided by one serving for the average adult man or woman aged 19–49 years (see also pages 156–158):

✓✓✓	or excellent	at least 50% (half)
✓✓	or good	25–50% (one-quarter to one-half)
✓	or useful	10–25% (one-tenth to one-quarter)

Note that recipes contribute other nutrients, but the analyses only include those that provide at least 10% RNI per portion. Vitamins and minerals where deficiencies are rare are not included.

Ⓥ denotes that a recipe is suitable for vegetarians.

Healthy Baking

Nutritious, wholesome and comforting

FOR MANY PEOPLE, BAKING REPRESENTS the essence of home life, with flavours and aromas that evoke some of the happiest memories of childhood. Hardly surprising, then, that a baking session – and eating the results! – is a relaxation, a comfort and a unique pleasure. So it's good news that a passion for baking can also be good for your health. Bread is one of the best and most versatile sources of starchy carbohydrate and also provides many vitamins and minerals. Cakes, biscuits and other sweet baked goods can be nourishing, too, both for the body and for the soul. Those you bake yourself will taste better than bought baked goods, and will be more nutritious.

Baking for a healthy diet

A lot of people believe that if they want to eat healthily, one of the things they have to give up is carbohydrate foods such as cakes, biscuits and even bread. But such sacrifices just aren't necessary. All these foods fit well into a healthy eating regime, and in fact contribute many important nutrients to your diet.

A little of what you fancy

Though most people think of cakes, biscuits and other baked goods as being high in fat and/or sugar, this is not always the case. The following pages demonstrate how easy it is to bake nutritious and delicious cakes, biscuits, scones, muffins and sweet breads, minimising the amount of fat and sugar without compromising on taste or texture. They also show you how to add extra nutrients to your baking by choosing ingredients carefully and including fruit and even vegetables.

Moderation, balance and variety are the 3 key words for healthy eating, and following these guidelines will mean that cakes, biscuits, muffins and other sweet baked goods can be included in your daily diet and make a positive contribution to your health.
* Moderate the amount of sweet baked goods you eat, and save rich cakes for special occasions rather than for every day.
* Balance your intake of baked goods with other types of food – for example, serve fresh fruit with a slice of teabread to make a well-rounded snack, or drink milk or fruit juice when enjoying a biscuit or muffin.
* Vary your diet as much as possible to include all the different types of food – starchy carbohydrates such as pasta, rice, and potatoes and other starchy vegetables as well as bread; protein-rich lean meat and poultry, dairy products, fish and pulses; fruit and vegetables; and grains, nuts and seeds.

While baked goods can be high in calories, it's worth remembering that not everyone needs to watch their weight – 6% of the population are clinically too thin and find it hard to put on weight. There are also times in everyone's life when poor appetites need stimulating – for example, faddy-eating phases in childhood; illness or convalescence; or as we get older. At such times, a piece of cake, a scone or a couple of home-made biscuits may be just what is needed.

A spoonful of sugar

Sugar isn't quite the demon that it has been made out to be in the past. There is a link between sugar and tooth decay, but nutritional guidelines suggest that the unhealthiest way to take sugar is between meals, in the form of sugary drinks and sweets that are sucked or chewed. Sugar as part of a healthy overall product – for example, a teacake or muffin – is much better, because it is less likely to cause tooth decay and the overall product has nutritional benefits.

Sugar is a necessary part of most sweet baking. It improves the flavour, 'mouth feel' and texture of cakes and adds bulk. And it is a natural preservative, helping to prevent baked goods from going rancid, mouldy or stale.

Home-made cakes, biscuits and sweet breads can serve as useful alternatives to confectionery for children – or for anyone with a sweet tooth. Most bought sweets contain little other than sugar and artificial flavourings, whereas the recipes in this book for cakes and other sweet things are as low in sugar as possible, and rich in nutrients.

Spotlight on bread

Bread is not described as the staff of life for nothing. One of the earliest 'recipes' known to mankind, and eaten in parts of the world (as flatbread) for thousands of years, bread deserves its reputation as an indispensable part of our diet.

Eating several slices of good-quality bread a day is an easy and delicious way to take in a high proportion of our daily supply of energy and vitamins – especially the important B-group vitamins, which help to regulate the nervous system, convert food into energy, and perform many more tasks. Most breads also contain useful amounts of iron, calcium and other minerals, and can provide extra vitamins and minerals by including ingredients such as fruit, vegetables, nuts and seeds.

For lunch or supper, make a yeasted pizza dough base and top with a rich tomato sauce, anchovies, olives and mozzarella (see page 126), or enjoy a mug of soup with savoury ricotta and fresh herb scones (see page 80)

A valuable source of nutrients

The main ingredients used to make breads, cakes and biscuits provide many nutrients and other beneficial compounds.

- Carbohydrates are the body's most important and easily used source of energy. Current guidelines are that carbohydrates should account for at least half our daily calorie intake, and that most of these calories should be from starchy foods. Nutritionally speaking, flours consist mostly of starchy carbohydrates.

- Fibre is provided by unrefined flours such as wholemeal and by wholegrains. Wholemeal flour supplies mainly insoluble fibre, which helps to prevent constipation; grains such as oats provide soluble fibre to help regulate blood sugar levels.

Refined flours are lower in fibre, but still contain some useful nutrients, and are enriched further by law.

- Fat-soluble vitamins A and D, needed for healthy vision and for growth, are found in butter, while oils extracted from olives, nuts and seeds contain the so-called essential fatty acids, as well as vitamin E.

- Protein for muscle building and for body repair and maintenance is supplied by eggs and milk, which also offer a range of vitamins and minerals such as calcium and iron.

- Phytochemicals, important substances found in most plant foods which help to fight disease, are found in fruit and vegetables. These foods also provide other valuable nutrients such as the antioxidants vitamin C and beta-carotene.

Why home-made is best

It's worth rediscovering the joys of home baking – not only will your family's health benefit if you bake wisely, ensuring your breads and cakes are rich in nutrients, but it's a relaxing activity for adults and fun for children.

Making time for baking

Baking was a traditional household skill for hundreds of years, particularly after sugar became readily available in the 18th century. But in the past 50 years or so, it has gradually become less common. Today in busy households, there may be little time for anything but the most basic or speedy cooking, while the huge growth in the commercial production of breads, cakes and biscuits has made home baking a luxury rather than a necessity.

Recently, though, with the growing emphasis on healthy, natural foods, we have started to discover the joys – and the benefits – of baking all over again. We bake by choice now, rather than from necessity, and it's no longer seen as an exclusively female activity. It's rewarding for anyone who wants to relax in the kitchen (baking a cake or a loaf is much less stressful than cooking a family dinner) and nurture their loved ones with a few home-made treats. Not least of the benefits is that when we've baked a cake or loaf of bread, it encourages us to sit down as a family to share and enjoy it, rather than just grabbing something to eat 'on the hoof'. In other words, baking has social benefits within the family. And it's not just the eating, but the act of baking, too. If you have children they will look forward to a weekly baking session. It's fun, creative and not difficult at all.

Even if you are busy, a regular baking session can usually be slotted into your schedule without too much trouble – perhaps on an evening when there is little to watch on TV or a wet Sunday in winter? Don't get bored, get baking!

What's in the cakes we buy?

Baking can really benefit from being done on a small scale rather than by mass-production methods. Even high-quality bought baked goods rarely taste as good as the home-made equivalent, and they certainly don't have that home-baked aroma. And few commercial cakes or biscuits can compare nutritionally with those you can make at home.

Just pick up a packet sponge cake or chocolate cake in the supermarket and read the list of ingredients. You'll soon realise that there is a lot more to a commercial cake than you may have thought.

Here are the main disadvantages of bought bakes:
* There is usually an overload of sugar in packet cakes and biscuits. This is partly to bulk out the item and reduce the production cost (thus increasing the profit) and partly because sugar helps to preserve long-life goods.
* The fats used in commercial baked goods are often the less healthy types – margarines and others that contain a particular type of fatty acid known as trans fats. These are created when vegetable oils are hardened (or hydrogenated) in the factory to make them suitable for commercial baking. Research shows that trans fats pose more risks to health than saturated fat (the kind found mainly in meat and dairy products).
* Long-life cakes and biscuits usually contain a substantial list of artificial additives – preservatives, flavourings and colourings. Some people believe that many of these additives can cause behavioural problems and allergic reactions in susceptible children.
* Commercial cakes and biscuits are less likely to include large quantities of nutritious ingredients such as wholegrains, fruits, nuts, seeds and so on, to keep costs down.

When you bake cakes, biscuits and other sweet items at home you can control the ingredients, the proportions and the method. You can choose healthier fats, in smaller quantities, and use less sugar. You can add plenty of 'plus factors' to make your baking even more nutritious. And the end result will almost always be less expensive and will taste wonderful.

A home-made loaf

There are some types of bread that aren't really worth trying to make at home, either because they are too complex or need special equipment. French bread is a good example – even in France, people leave that to the baker! But apart from these exceptions, bread is well worth making at home.

Home-baked bread will usually be richer in nutrients than bought loaves, especially if made with wholegrain flours, particularly those that are stoneground, as well as good-quality oils, and extras such as nuts, seeds and dried fruits. And, like home-made cakes and biscuits, your own bread will be free from preservatives and other artificial additives, such as flour improvers. Finally, the eating qualities of home-made bread are superior to most commercial loaves as they tend to be denser, containing less water or air, weight for weight, and so are more satisfying for longer.

▲ A tempting selection for tea-time (from top left): Gingerbread (see page 34), Blackcurrant teabread (see page 152), Fudgy brownies (see page 102), Drop scones (see page 74) and Fig rolls (see page 100)

◀ Good ways to start the day: toasted slices of Quick wholemeal bread (see page 110) with jam, or energy-boosting Breakfast muffins (see page 66)

healthy baking

13

Flours for good baking

Flour is the basis of every loaf of bread and virtually every cake. There are many different types of flour and your choice is vital for the success of your home baking, as well as important in nutritional terms.

Wheat flours

A huge percentage of the flours used in baking is made from wheat, the staple grain of Europe and, indeed, much of the Western world.

Brown flour (also called wheatmeal flour) contains about 85% of the whole grain, and therefore a similar percentage of its nutrients. It produces a lighter bread than wholemeal flour.

Granary flour is a wheatmeal (brown) flour made from malted wheat (grains that have been allowed to start germinating), and it contains cracked (kibbled) and whole wheat grains, and sometimes rye flour. Its nutritional benefits are similar to those of brown flour.

Plain (white) flour became available as a consequence of the modern milling methods invented over 100 years ago, whereby the starchy endosperm of the grain can be separated from the bran and the germ, which are discarded, leaving 72–74% of the whole grain. In the UK, by law, some of the nutrients that are removed in this milling process (vitamin B_1, niacin, iron and calcium) are artificially returned to the flour before it is sold. However, the fibre and protein content of white flour will be lower than that of wholemeal flour. If you want to avoid the heaviness of wholemeal bread and cakes, a good compromise is to use a mixture of white and wholemeal flours.

Plain white flour usually has a low gluten content, resulting in a crumbly texture that is good for baking cakes and biscuits but not suitable for bread. You can sometimes find an even finer flour for cake-making, which contains only 50–65% of the wheat grain.

Self-raising flour has raising agents added to it after the milling process – usually a mixture of bicarbonate of soda and cream of tartar (tartaric acid). Both white and wholemeal self-raising flours are available.

Spelt is an ancient ancestor of wheat, containing more protein, B vitamins and iron than normal wheat, but less gluten.

Stoneground flour (usually wholemeal) is milled by traditional methods rather than modern factory roller-mills. Milling with modern metal rollers creates heat, which spoils some of the nutrients – particularly the B vitamins and the essential fats. Stonegrinding keeps the grain cool and preserves almost all of the nutrients. Stoneground flour is usually coarser and heavier

wholemeal flour   plain (white) flour   Granary flour   spelt flour   rye flour   buckwheat flour   cornmeal

than factory-milled flour, so bread made from it may need a longer rising time or a little extra yeast to leaven it.

Strong flour, sometimes labelled 'bread' flour, is milled from hard wheat, which is high in gluten. It is gluten that helps dough to stretch and expand, and therefore to rise, so strong flour is ideal for bread-making. Both white and wholemeal bread flours are available.

Wholemeal flour (also called wholewheat flour) contains the whole of the grain – the bran (outer layers), the endosperm (starch middle part) and the germ (the embryo plant at the base of the grain) – and therefore retains most of its nutrients. It is high in B vitamins and a range of nutritionally important minerals, including magnesium, iron and selenium. It is also high in fibre and is a reasonable source of protein (12.7 g in each 100 g/3½ oz), as well as containing some essential fats. Breads and cakes made with 100% wholemeal flour will be heavier than those made with refined flours, and their keeping properties may be reduced because of their higher fat content.

Non-wheat flours

Baking with flours milled from grains and cereals other than wheat, and from vegetables and nuts, will bring variety to your breads and other baked goods, and may offer different nutritional benefits. When using these flours you need to consider their baking properties, as they all contain less gluten than wheat flour and some contain no gluten at all. So they usually need to be mixed with wheat flour to prevent the finished bread from being too dense and heavy.

rice flour   potato flour   soya flour

Gluten-free and wheat-free baking

Gluten is a protein found in wheat and rye; a similar type of protein is found in barley and oats. Gluten intolerance causes coeliac disease, an inflammatory condition of the gastrointestinal tract. Another intolerance is to the wheat grain, which can then cause an allergic reaction.

Specially produced gluten-free and wheat-free commercial breads and baked goods are available now, as are specially blended gluten and wheat-free flour mixtures. However, there are various types of flour that you can use in breads and baking that are naturally gluten-free (see Non-wheat flours, below) and wheat-free. Although these tend to produce denser, heavier breads and baked goods than those made with wheat flours, they can be full of flavour and very satisfying. Most gluten-free breads are risen with bicarbonate of soda or baking powder, as yeast needs gluten to make bread dough rise.

Buckwheat flour, milled from a nutty-tasting grain, is rich in protein and offers useful amounts of iron. It is gluten-free.

Cornmeal (also called maizemeal or polenta), usually rich yellow in colour, may be coarse or medium. Cornflour, a very fine white flour milled from the heart of the maize kernel, is used mainly as a thickener. Both cornmeal and cornflour are gluten-free and similar to wheat flour nutritionally.

Oat flour contains few vitamins and minerals in significant quantities, but it is high in soluble fibre, which can help to reduce high blood cholesterol levels.

Potato flour is high in starchy carbohydrate and gluten-free.

Rice flour, which has a fairly bland flavour, can be used in many types of baked goods. It is gluten-free. It has slightly less protein and fibre than white wheat flour.

Rye flour makes well-flavoured bread with a chewy texture. It can be used alone to make an acceptably risen loaf, but is normally mixed with wheat flour. Dark rye flour is a useful source of B vitamins, vitamin E, iron, copper, zinc and fibre. Light rye flours contain proportionally fewer of these nutrients.

Soya flour is made from raw or toasted soya beans (toasted has a better flavour). It is high in protein and gluten-free.

In addition to these non-wheat flours, flour for baking is also milled from barley, millet, chickpeas and chestnuts.

healthy baking

15

Fats, eggs and dairy products

Fats and oils, eggs and dairy products such as milk and yogurt are used to enrich baked goods of all kinds and improve their keeping qualities. Here's how to choose the best of these ingredients to use for healthy baking.

Fats and oils

Nutritionally, fats and oils consist of several different types of 'fatty acid' plus glycerol. Fatty acids can be broken down into 3 groups:

Saturated fatty acids occur in the largest quantities in fats that are hard at room temperature – lard, suet, butter and, of course, fatty cuts of meat, cheese and other full-fat dairy products. Saturated fat is an acceptable part of a healthy diet, in moderation – high intakes increase levels of harmful LDL (low-density lipoprotein) cholesterol in the blood, and this can lead to an increased risk of heart disease and stroke.

Monounsaturated fatty acids occur in the largest quantities in fats that are liquid at room temperature, such as olive oil and groundnut oil, and in avocados and many nuts. These fats have a beneficial effect by lowering LDL cholesterol levels in the blood and raising the level of another, beneficial type of cholesterol, HDL (high-density lipoprotein). This helps to remove the LDL cholesterol from the blood and deliver it to the liver for excretion.

Polyunsaturated fatty acids are found in the largest quantities in fats that are liquid even when kept cold, such as sunflower oil and safflower oil. These fats are excellent at helping to lower LDL cholesterol levels in the blood. However, if eaten in excess, they will actually lower the good HDL cholesterol levels too, so moderation is the key.

Polyunsaturated fats contain the 'essential fatty acids' – omega-3 and omega-6 – which are needed for good health. These essential fats may help to prevent or control a wide range of ailments and diseases, such as heart disease, cancer, arthritis, Alzheimer's, skin complaints and pre-menstrual syndrome.

Butter versus margarine

Many nutritionists believe that butter, a pure, natural fat containing useful amounts of the important fat-soluble vitamins A and D, is better for your health than commercial hydrogenated margarines. This is because the hydrogenating process (which turns vegetable, seed or fish oils into hard fat) changes some of their unsaturated fats into trans fatty acids or 'trans fats'. These trans fats are thought to be more harmful than saturated fats in the diet, as they appear not only to raise LDL blood cholesterol levels but also to reduce HDL levels. Butter, on the other hand, raises LDL levels but maintains – or even slightly raises – the levels of good HDL in the blood, especially when used in combination with wholemeal flours and wholegrains. In addition, butter gives baked goods a wonderful flavour, much better than margarine.

If you want to use margarine instead of butter, choose one labelled 'high in monounsaturates'. These are usually based on olive oil, and they contain few, if any, trans fats (they may even be labelled as such).

Low-fat spreads may also contain high levels of trans fats. In addition, they have a high water content, as do soft tub margarines, so both should only be used in recipes specially devised for them.

Oils for good health

Oils pressed from fruit and vegetables, seeds and nuts can be good sources of several nutrients, in particular vitamin E, an antioxidant that helps to prevent heart disease and other ailments. Vitamin E is not easy to get in the diet, so using oil in your baking can make a valuable contribution.

Olive oil is often used in breads, especially Mediterranean-style loaves. Many olive oils have a fairly strong flavour, which makes them less suitable for sweet baking.

Sunflower oil is a good choice for cakes, biscuits and other

sweet bakes. It is light in colour, with a mild, bland flavour.
Corn, safflower and corn oils can be used in the same way as
sunflower oil.

The benefits of eggs

A medium-sized egg contains about 90 kcal and 7 g fat,
roughly two-thirds of which is monounsaturated and the rest
saturated. Eggs contain no sugars and are a good source of
protein. They also offer a wide variety of vitamins and
minerals, being a good source of vitamins A, D, E and the
B group (especially B_{12} and folate) and of iron and iodine.

Besides being nutrient-rich, eggs are a vital ingredient in
many forms of baking, adding flavour and colour as well as
lightness of texture. Whisked egg whites, folded into a mixture
before baking, help a cake to rise, as do whole eggs whisked
vigorously with sugar until thick and creamy.

Nutritious dairy products

Most dairy products are excellent sources of protein, calcium,
and vitamins A and B, and can also make a reasonable
contribution to zinc and vitamin D intake. Full-fat dairy
products can be high in saturated fats, but there are many
natural lower-fat alternatives that are ideal to use when baking.
Buttermilk was traditionally the liquid whey that remained after
cream had been churned into butter, but nowadays it is often
made by adding bacterial cultures to skimmed milk. As such it
is low in fat, and has a pleasant tangy flavour. If you are
unable to find buttermilk, you can 'sour' 240 ml (8 fl oz) milk
by stirring in 1 tbsp lemon juice or 2 tsp cream of tartar and
leaving it for 5 minutes.
Cream when whipped is a popular filling for sandwich cakes
and meringues. As most creams are high in saturated fat, it's a
good idea to opt for those that are the lowest in fat and
calories (whipping cream is a better choice than double or
clotted cream) or to mix cream with lower-fat yogurt – half
whipped whipping cream and half plain low-fat or Greek-style
yogurt sweetened with a little clear honey or icing sugar is
delicious. Another idea is to substitute a creamy alternative
such as ricotta cheese, fromage frais or half-fat crème fraîche
beaten with a little icing sugar.
Milk enriches and lightens the texture of teabreads, teacakes,
scones and batters. Semi-skimmed milk, which is 1.6% fat (as

Eggs and dairy products, such as milk, cheese, yogurt and
buttermilk, are nutritious ingredients for baking, contributing
valuable protein, vitamins and minerals

opposed to whole milk, with 3.9% fat), is suitable for use in
most baking recipes, and has a mild, creamy quality.
Yogurt, like buttermilk, adds a delicious tang to baked goods.
Plain low-fat yogurt contains 0.8% fat, as does low-fat bio
yogurt. Standard Greek-style yogurt has a higher fat content
(7.5%). It makes a good alternative to cream in cake fillings.
Hard cheeses can be high in fat (Cheddar cheese has 34 g fat
per 100 g/3½ oz; Parmesan has 33 g fat for the same weight),
but only a small amount is needed to enrich and add flavour to
savoury breads and scones. Lower-fat cheeses, such as feta
(20 g fat per 100 g/3½ oz) and goat's cheese (14.5 g), can be
used very successfully too.
Soft fresh cheeses vary in fat content from 47% for cream
cheese to 11% for ricotta and 8% for standard fromage frais.
A cream cheese icing is traditional for carrot cake, but ricotta
and fromage frais both make good alternatives. They also
work well as a substitute for buttercream (butter beaten with
eggs and sugar).

Sugars and other sweeteners

Although sugar and the majority of other sweeteners provide lots of calories and almost no nutrients, they are an essential part of most cakes, biscuits, teabreads and sweet yeasted breads. In healthy baking, the aim is to reduce quantities to produce a lower-calorie result, but without compromising on taste and ultimate satisfaction.

Refined sugars
Refined white sugar is 99.9% pure sucrose, produced from sugar cane or sugar beet plants at the factory. It contains no vitamins and minerals, just calories for instant energy.
Caster sugar has fine grains and is the white sugar of choice for sponge cakes as well as cakes that require a light texture or colour or are prepared by creaming butter and sugar together. Caster sugar is also used for meringues.
Granulated sugar comes in fairly large granules. It can be used for rubbed-in mixtures such as biscuits.
Icing sugar has been ground to a fine powder. It is useful for icings and fillings and for dusting over cakes.
Soft brown sugar, whether light or dark, is simply refined white sugar that has been tossed in syrup or molasses to colour it.

Unrefined sugars
Unrefined, or 'natural', sugars come from raw sugar cane. They retain a proportion of the molasses – the brown residue from refining that contains the nutrients of the sugar cane. In general, the darker the sugar, the more molasses it contains, and the more flavour and nutrients. Unrefined sugars have more flavour than refined sugar, and may be less sweet.
Demerara sugar is a rich and deep gold and has large, slightly sticky crystals. It can be used in tray bakes, rock cakes and biscuits, and for sweet yeasted breads.
Golden granulated and golden caster sugar, pale gold in colour, can be used instead of their white counterparts. They will add extra flavour, but the end result may be slightly darker and very slightly heavier.
Molasses sugar is soft, moist and fine-textured and has a strong flavour.
Muscovado sugar is very soft and fine in texture, and may be either light brown or dark brown, when it is sometimes called Barbados sugar. Muscovado sugar is excellent in fruit cakes.

Syrups and purées for sweetening
Golden syrup, refined from the sap of the sugar cane, is less sweet than sugar. It contains no significant nutrients, just

Sugar is an essential ingredient in most sweet baking.
From the left: demerara sugar, dark molasses sugar, icing sugar, light muscovado sugar, golden caster sugar and caster sugar

Fruit purées as fat/sugar substitutes

Dried fruits and fresh fruit such as apples can be turned into a purée and used in baking recipes to replace some of the sugar and fat. They provide natural sweetness, moistness and a delicious flavour.

Purées work particularly well in teabreads and fruit cakes, but they are not suitable for cakes such as sponges, where the proportion of fat to sugar is crucial to the rise and texture of the finished cake. Fresh apple purée is ideal in lighter-coloured cakes and bakes, while dried fruit purées can be used in darker rich fruit cakes. Prune purée is wonderful in chocolate cake.

To use the purées in baking, the simplest method is to replace half the fat and half the sugar with the same weight of fruit purée. For example, if a recipe calls for 100 g (3½ oz) each sugar and butter, use 50 g (1¾ oz) each sugar and butter plus 100 g (3½ oz) fruit purée. You can, of course, replace less of the fat and sugar with fruit purée, or replace either the fat or the sugar. Experimenting will show you which result you like best.

● To make dried fruit purée, roughly chop 100 g (3½ oz) ready-to-eat prunes, dried apricots, dried apples and so on, put them in a pan with enough water to cover, then cover and simmer until very soft. Purée in a blender or food processor.

● To make apple purée, peel, core and thinly slice dessert apples, put into a saucepan and add 1 tbsp water per apple. Cover and simmer very gently for about 30 minutes or until tender. Mash or purée in a blender or food processor.

Syrups and fruit purées can also be used to sweeten baked goods. From the left: apple purée, maple syrup, golden syrup, malt extract, molasses and clear honey

calories. It adds softness, moistness and stickiness to the cakes and biscuits in which it is used.

Honey is made by the bee in its 'honey stomach' and in the hive, using nectar collected from flowers. Depending on where the nectar has been gathered, honey flavours can vary, for example from strong eucalyptus or lavender to delicate clover or lime blossom. Clear honey, with a runny texture, can be used as a sweetener in baking, although being much sweeter than sugar you need less of it. Honey contains only minute amounts of nutrients.

Malt extract, a concentrated extract of germinated barley, has a pleasant, distinctive, sweet flavour. It provides good quantities of phosphorus and is a useful source of magnesium.

Maple syrup, extracted from the sap of the maple tree, can be used in similar ways to golden syrup. Delicious and fragrant, it contains useful amounts of zinc.

Molasses, a by-product of sugar refining, has a very strong flavour that can be slightly bitter (the darker the molasses, the less sugar it contains). It is a useful source of vitamin B_6 and magnesium as well as providing some iron and calcium. It can be refined to produce black treacle, which is still rich in the molasses nutrients. Smallish amounts of molasses can be used in gingerbreads and rich fruit cakes to add sweetness, colour, flavour and a sticky texture.

Concentrated fruit purées and juices, such as apple concentrate, can be used as a sweetener in baking, especially in recipes made by the melting method. All fruits, and many vegetables, contain natural 'intrinsic' sugars (sugars that are part of the natural cellular structure of the plant). It is thought that these sugars may be better for you than refined or 'extrinsic' sugars (which include raw cane sugar, syrups and honey) because they may be less likely to cause fluctuations in blood sugar levels, and may also be less likely to cause tooth decay. (For more on using fruit and vegetables as sweeteners in baking, see above and page 22.)

Yeasts and other raising agents

Raising or leavening agents are essential to give breads and cakes their characteristic lightness and texture. Yeast is used for kneaded bread doughs, while other raising agents such as bicarbonate of soda and baking powder are added to 'quick' breads (soda bread, for example), scones, muffins and many cakes.

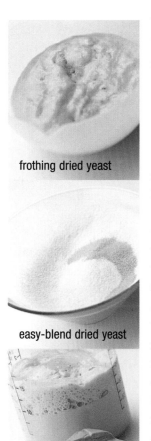

frothing dried yeast

easy-blend dried yeast

fresh yeast

Yeast

Yeast is a living organism. In a moist, warm environment and when fed with sugar and starch, yeast ferments to produce carbon dioxide, and it is this that makes bread doughs rise. Dried yeast is alive but dormant because of the lack of moisture. Yeast is a useful source of B vitamins.

Dried yeast is bought as granules, in individual sachets or tubs. It is usually mixed with a little tepid water, often with a pinch of sugar to help reactivate it, and then left in a warm place for 15 minutes or until a frothy head has formed. The mixture is then ready to add to the flour. Dried yeast can be kept in a cool, dry place for up to 6 months.

Easy-blend dried yeast (also called fast-action dried yeast) is quicker and more convenient to use than ordinary dried yeast, as it does not have to be dissolved in liquid but is sprinkled straight into the flour. In theory, only one rising is required with easy-blend yeast, saving even more time, but in practice a better result is obtained if you give the dough the traditional 2 risings. Easy-blend yeast can be kept as for dried yeast.

Fresh yeast can be bought from bakers who bake bread on the premises, as well as from healthfood shops and supermarkets. Like ordinary dried yeast, it needs to be mixed with tepid liquid first and left to become frothy. Fresh yeast can be kept, loosely wrapped, in the fridge for up to 3 days, or it can be frozen in suitable-sized pieces for up to 4 months (leave it to thaw before using).

Wild yeasts are microscopic spores that are naturally present in flour and floating in the air. They have been used successfully to raise doughs for over 6000 years, and produce bread that has a delicious tangy, slightly sour flavour. A mixture of flour and tepid water (the 'starter') is left to ferment, at room temperature, for several days, being 'fed' regularly with more flour and water, until it is bubbling, which indicates that the wild yeasts have been activated. Once created, a starter can be kept going almost indefinitely and used for regular baking.

Other raising agents

The usual method of raising most cake mixtures, quick bread doughs and batters is by the inclusion of baking powder or bicarbonate of soda. Just as with yeast, these produce carbon dioxide gas bubbles, which expand during baking. Contact with moisture creates the carbon dioxide, so once mixed the cake or bread should be baked without delay. Both baking powder and bicarbonate of soda can be kept in an airtight container in a cool, dry place for up to 6 months.

Baking powder is a combination of bicarbonate of soda and and an acid such as cream of tartar. Self-raising flour contains baking powder as well as salt.

Bicarbonate of soda can be used as a raising agent on its own as long as the recipe includes an acidic ingredient, such as vinegar, soured cream, buttermilk or yogurt.

bicarbonate of soda

Flavourings for variety

Whether it's a sprinkling of herbs or spice seeds on a loaf of bread or a spoonful of ground cinnamon or vanilla extract in a batch of muffins or biscuits, a little flavouring will give zest and variety to your baking.

Alcohol

A spoonful or two of rum, brandy or sherry will enhance the flavour of fruit cakes or the dried fruit can be soaked in the alcohol first; simple sponge cakes can be made special by drizzling over a little fruit-flavoured liqueur. Alcohol is fat-free and the calories these tiny amounts contribute to your diet will be minimal.

Chocolate

Chocolate is high in calories, sugar and fat (530 kcals, 56 g sugar and 30 g fat per 100 g/3½ oz), but it's not all bad news – dark chocolate also contains useful amounts of iron, plus an antioxidant that can help to prevent the build-up of harmful LDL cholesterol. Just a little good-quality chocolate is needed to add richness to sweet baking. When buying chocolate,

always check the percentage of cocoa solids it contains. The higher the content (at least 70%), the better the chocolate, and the less added fat and sugar it will contain.

Cocoa powder is another way to add chocolate flavour, and without the calories – 2 rounded tbsp contain 62 kcals and only 4.5 g fat.

Herbs and spices

Chopped fresh or dried herbs can be mixed into yeasted and quick bread doughs and mixtures for savoury muffins and scones for a flavoursome result, or the herbs can be sprinkled on top before baking. Basil, thyme, marjoram and chives are all delicious, as are rosemary and sage added more sparingly.

Spices can be used in both sweet and savoury baking. Whole seeds, such as fennel, caraway and cumin, are good additions to savoury breads as well as some cakes and biscuits, mixed in or sprinkled over the top. Ground coriander and chilli can spice up breads, savoury muffins and tortillas, while ground cinnamon, nutmeg, ginger, allspice, cloves and mixed spice are traditional flavourings for cakes and biscuits and sweet breads.

Salt

Salt is an indispensable ingredient in bread because it helps to toughen the gluten and make a good rise; it also improves the flavour – a loaf made without salt can taste quite bland. Surprisingly, salt brings out flavours in sweet baking too. Even a pinch can make a difference. The small quantity needed won't affect the total amount of salt in your diet. Home-baked breads and cakes contain less salt than commercial ones.

Vanilla

Vanilla adds a delicate flavour to plain sponges and biscuits as well as to icings. Always buy good-quality pure vanilla extract, which is distilled from vanilla pods, rather than vanilla essence or vanilla flavouring, both synthetic products that may not contain any vanilla at all. Using vanilla sugar is another way to add this flavouring to baked goods. To make your own vanilla sugar, push a vanilla pod into a container of sugar and leave for at least a week. The pod can be removed and reused, or left in the container, topping up the sugar as it is used.

healthy baking

Fruit, vegetables, nuts and seeds

Fruits and vegetables should be included in your diet every day, while nuts and seeds are nutritious foods that are beneficial if eaten regularly. Baking provides an opportunity to enjoy all of these in imaginative ways.

Sweet fruity goodness

Most fresh fruits are high in fibre, vitamin C and minerals such as potassium (which helps to prevent high blood pressure). Orange-fleshed fruits, such as mangoes, peaches, apricots, plums and papaya, also provide the important antioxidant beta-carotene, while other fruits add their own beneficial contributions: raspberries are a good source of folate, bananas offer useful amounts of vitamin B_6 and blackberries are the richest fruit source of vitamin E.

All fruits contain fructose, a natural or 'intrinsic' sugar that is part of the cellular structure of the plant. Adding fruit to cakes and bakes is a heathier way to satisfy a sweet tooth than using refined sugar alone, as sugar provides only calories with no nutrients. With some sweet fruit in the mixture you can cut down the amount of sugar you include. And, in addition to sweetness, fruit will also contribute flavour, texture, moisture and satisfying bulk.

Dried fruits are a particularly good way to add sweetness to baking – the drying process removes much of the moisture from fruit, leaving a higher concentration of fructose, so they taste sweeter. Many dried fruits are good sources of fibre, and most offer minerals such as iron, calcium, potassium and magnesium as well as B vitamins.

Versatile and nutritious vegetables

A surprisingly wide variety of vegetables is suitable for use in baking, both sweet and savoury, and in so many unexpected ways. Vegetables can provide sweetness or a savoury flavour, add crunch or a smooth texture, increase moisture and so on. Using vegetables in breads, cakes and other baking will increase their nutritional content too.

Most vegetables are a good source of vitamin C, fibre and potassium. Brightly coloured carrots, tomatoes, peppers, orange-fleshed pumpkin and other squash, and sweet potatoes offer beta-carotene; potatoes and parsnips contain a variety of B vitamins; leafy green vegetables such as spinach provide folate; and tomatoes supply lycopene, a powerful antioxidant.

Vegetables work well in savoury yeasted breads, either added to the dough or used as a topping or filling. For example, focaccia is traditionally flavoured with vegetables such as sun-dried tomatoes, onions and garlic, and pizzas are delicious topped with roast vegetables such as red onion and aubergine. A wholemeal loaf can be enhanced by kneading grated vegetables such as courgettes into the dough, or a light quick bread can be made with mashed potato or pumpkin.

On the sweet side, grated carrots are essential in irresistible carrot cake, and parsnips and beetroots can be used in fruit cakes. Puréed cooked sweet potato is a delicious and colourful addition to teabreads and muffins.

Healthy fats from nuts and seeds

All seeds and nuts – apart from chestnuts – are high in fat (about 60–70 g per 100 g/3½ oz), and therefore calories, but the fat they contain is mostly the unsaturated kind that is good for your health. Nuts are high in monounsaturated fat, while seeds are higher in polyunsaturated fat. Both nuts and seeds contribute good amounts of the essential fatty acids to the diet, as well as protein, B vitamins, vitamin E, iron, zinc and magnesium. They also contain fibre.

It is a good idea to keep small quantities of several kinds of nuts and seeds in your larder because they are so versatile in baking. Walnuts, pecans, almonds and hazelnuts are the most frequently used nuts, with brazils, cashews and macadamia nuts being less common but just as delicious. Sunflower seeds, pumpkin seeds, sesame seeds, poppy seeds and linseeds also have many uses.

Children under 5 years old should not be given whole nuts because of the risk of choking; ground nuts are fine.

► Bake an upside-down sponge with juicy mango slices (see page 48)

▼ Flavour savoury scones with watercress and Cheddar (see page 78)

▲ Add crunchy almonds to twice-baked Italian biscuits (see page 92)

◄ Give a multigrain loaf more texture with mixed seeds (see page 108)

Baking basics

The keys to successful baking are simple: measure ingredients carefully, use the size of tin suggested in the recipe and check the accuracy of your oven. Here are a few more tips for making breads, cakes and biscuits.

Bread basics

If you are making a yeasted bread, you'll find that almost all recipes follow the same basic procedure: mixing in the yeast (see page 20), kneading the dough, rising and shaping.

Kneading the dough

Once the yeast, flour and liquid (plus any other ingredients specified in the recipe) have been mixed together to make a dough that leaves the bowl clean, it is time for kneading. The kneading process gives a yeast dough elasticity, develops and strengthens the gluten, and ensures the bread will rise evenly.

Turn the dough out onto a lightly floured surface. Using the heel of your hand, push the dough away from you, to stretch it out, then fold the side farthest away back towards you, rolling the dough into a loose ball. Turn the dough slightly, then stretch it out again. Continue kneading like this for about 10 minutes. (Rather than kneading by hand, you can use a heavy-duty electric mixer fitted with a dough hook.)

Thinking of buying a bread-making machine?

Some people, especially beginners, find bread-making machines excellent, as they remove the 'need to knead'. However, they also remove most of the fun and sense of creativity that you get with traditional bread-making, and experienced home bakers generally find that loaves made in a machine cannot be as versatile, and are not quite as good to eat, as those made by hand.

The first rise

Shape the dough into a smooth ball and put it into a lightly oiled bowl. Cover to prevent a dry crust from forming, and leave to rise until doubled in size. This can be done in a warm place (about 30°C/86°F), which is the quickest, or in a cooler place such as at room temperature. The dough can even be left to rise in the fridge overnight.

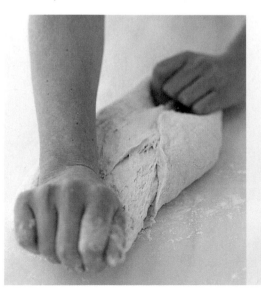

◀ Knead a yeasted dough by pushing and stretching it to develop the gluten; as you knead, the dough will gradually change in texture, becoming elastic, smooth and almost glossy

healthy baking

24

◄ To test if dough is properly risen, stick a finger into the centre; the indentation should remain after you pull your finger out

► For a tin loaf, press or roll out the dough into an oblong, then roll it up like a Swiss roll; tuck the ends under and place it gently in the greased tin

Shaping the loaf

Turn the risen dough out onto the lightly floured work surface again and 'knock it back' – punch it down with your fist to flatten it and expel excess air. Knead for 2–3 minutes to get it back to its original smooth texture, after which it is ready for shaping into loaves or rolls.

The simplest loaf shapes to make are balls, rounds and ovals, all of which are baked on a greased baking sheet. To shape dough to fit a loaf tin, flatten it to an oblong, making the short sides the same length as the tin, then roll up from a short side. Turn the roll so it is seam side down and tuck the ends under.

There are several more interesting shapes that are quite easy to make. For a spiral, shape the dough into a fat sausage, then curl it round itself, keeping it flat on the work surface. For a plait, divide the dough into 3 pieces and shape each one into a long, thin sausage. Press the top ends together, then plait together quite loosely. For shaping rolls, see Basic loaf, Some more ideas, page 107.

'Proving' and baking

Once shaped, most yeast doughs are left to rise again, or 'prove', before baking in a preheated oven. To test if a loaf is done, tap the base with your knuckle (if baked in a tin, tip the loaf out to test it). If the bread sounds hollow, like a drum, it is cooked. If it isn't ready, just return it to the oven (without the tin) and bake for a few more minutes, then test it again.

When the bread is done, leave it to cool on a wire rack for at least 2 hours before eating.

Freezing bread

Bread is very useful to have on hand in the freezer, and if you make your own it is well worth baking a large batch and then freezing some. Both yeasted breads and quick breads freeze extremely well, as long as they are tightly wrapped to prevent them from drying out. Plain loaves can be stored for up to 6 months, while enriched breads will keep for 3 months.

Most breads simply need thawing in their packaging at room temperature. Flat breads such as pittas, naan and tortillas benefit from being warmed after thawing: loosely wrap in foil and heat briefly in the oven before serving.

You can also freeze bread dough. The dough used for pizzas is a particularly handy standby. Make it but do not let it rise, then freeze in a sealed polythene bag; it can be kept for up to 1 month. Before use, re-seal the bag to allow space for rising, then leave in the fridge overnight. The next day, knock it back, shape and add the topping, then rise again briefly and bake.

Finishes for bread

Loaves and rolls can be glazed or sprinkled with a topping before baking to make them even more attractive and to add flavour.

- For a shiny, golden loaf, brush with beaten egg mixed with a pinch of salt.
- For a crusty top, brush with salt water.
- For a soft top, brush with milk.
- For a rustic loaf, dust lightly with wholemeal flour.
- Brush with beaten egg or oil, then top the loaf with seeds, such as poppy seeds (traditional for a plait), caraway or sesame seeds.
- Glaze with beaten egg, then sprinkle over a grain – oat flakes, cracked wheat and barley are all good.
- Sprinkle with grated hard cheese or chopped fresh herbs – a cheese-topped loaf is delicious with a vegetable soup.

▲ For the creaming method, beat soft butter with sugar until the mixture is almost like whipped cream

◄ For the rubbing-in method, rub cold butter into flour until the mixture resembles crumbs

▼ For whisked sponges, whisk eggs with sugar until thick enough to make a 'ribbon trail' on the surface

Cake and biscuit basics

There are 3 basic ways of making cake and biscuit mixtures: creaming, melting and rubbing-in. In addition, cakes can be lightened by folding in whisked egg whites or whisking eggs and sugar 'to the ribbon' (see below), or mixed by a quick all-in-one method (when the fat, sugar, eggs and flour are all put into a bowl together and whisked up).

For the creaming method, butter (at room temperature) is beaten with sugar until the mixture is pale, light and fluffy, before beaten eggs and flour are added. This is the traditional method for a Victoria sponge. For the melting method, used for gingerbread and some fruit cakes, the butter is warmed with the sugar until liquid, then eggs and flour are mixed in. For the rubbing-in method, cold firm butter is rubbed into the flour with the fingertips, just as when making pastry, and then sugar is added.

Whisking in air

Whisked sponges are the lightest of cakes. They often contain no added fat and only a small amount of flour, and depend on the air that is whisked in to achieve a rise. Very gentle heat is needed to help the whisking process – an electric mixer will create its own heat, but if you use a hand whisk or rotary beater, you will need to set the mixing bowl over a pan of hot, almost boiling water.

Put the eggs and sugar in the bowl and whisk them together vigorously until the mixture is very pale and has roughly tripled in volume. It should be so thick that when the whisk is lifted up, the mixture dropping from it holds its shape in a 'ribbon trail' on the surface of the mixture in the bowl. Once the flour has been gently folded in, the cake should be baked right away as the whisked mixture is very delicate.

Whisked egg whites

Another way to add air to a cake mixture is by folding in stiffly whisked egg whites. For best results, use the freshest of eggs, and when separating the egg yolks from the whites be sure that there is not even the tiniest trace of yolk left. If there is, the whites will not whisk to a stiff foam. Also, be sure that the bowl and beaters are completely clean and free of grease. Using an electric mixer is the quickest way to whisk whites to a stiff texture.

Preparing tins and baking sheets

Even if your cake tins and baking sheets are non-stick, it is a good idea to grease them. A mild-flavoured oil is an easy option – just paint it on sparingly with a pastry brush.

For most cakes you will also need to line the tin with baking parchment or greaseproof paper, either just on the bottom or on the sides too. This will help to prevent the outside of the cake from burning and makes it easier to turn it out after baking. All lining paper should be cut to fit exactly, otherwise the cake may have lumps and bumps in it. If you use greaseproof paper, you may need to brush it with oil. This isn't necessary with baking parchment.

For most biscuits, greasing the baking sheet is enough, but those that are rich will also need a lining of greaseproof paper or baking parchment, to prevent them from sticking. Another, very convenient option is a non-stick liner that can be wiped clean and used over and over again.

Baking cakes and biscuits

Depending on the type of cake or biscuit, you can test for doneness by pressing the centre lightly with the fingertips (whisked sponges should spring back, whereas other cakes and some biscuits will be just firm or quite firm to the touch), by inserting a skewer into the centre (it should come out clean in most cases, the exception being brownies) or by judging the colour and appearance (risen, golden brown and so on). Recipes specify how to tell if the cake or biscuits are cooked.

Once removed from the oven, most cakes are left to cool in the tin, either for a few minutes – before being turned out onto a wire rack – or completely. Whisked sponges should be removed from the tin straight away.

Biscuits can scorch easily, so it's a good idea to check them 5 minutes before the recommended baking time is up. Remember, too, that they will crisp up after they are removed from the oven, so you don't want to overbake them. Leave them on the baking sheets for a couple of minutes, then use a palette knife to transfer them to a wire rack to cool.

Freezing cakes and biscuits

Most cakes, scones, muffins and teabreads can be frozen without any deterioration in quality, but should be wrapped well to prevent moisture loss. To avoid damaging delicate

Use a pastry brush to grease tins and baking sheets lightly with oil, then if necessary line them; for muffins, use special paper cases

Wrap slices individually so they can be removed from the freezer when wanted

cakes, such as meringues and cheesecakes, it is a good idea to open freeze them first (i.e. freeze them unwrapped on a tray) until firm, then wrap them and return to the freezer.

Fillings or toppings made with cream, ricotta cheese, fromage frais or yogurt don't freeze well, and even simple glacé icings may crack in the freezer. Therefore, it's better to freeze the cake plain and fill or decorate it after thawing.

Biscuits store well in the freezer and are very quick to thaw. Some biscuit doughs (such as that for Digestive biscuits on page 84) can be frozen raw, wrapped in cling film or baking parchment and overwrapped in foil. Then when you want to bake the biscuits, remove the dough from the freezer and thaw until it can be sliced for baking.

Cakes for All Occasions

From tea-time treats to tempting desserts

YES, YOU CAN HAVE YOUR CAKE and eat it too! The cakes
in this chapter are every bit as delicious as you could
hope for, while containing wholesome ingredients to
boost your nutritional intake. For a special dessert, try a
feather-light Swiss roll, filled with fresh summer fruit,
cream and yogurt, or a rich and moist chocolate cake.
A creamy Italian rice cake is another tempting idea, as is
a spectacular hazelnut meringue.
Plainer options, such as banana
cake or gingerbread, make ideal
'cut-and-come-again' cakes, to
enjoy as a snack or in a lunchbox.

Summer fruit Swiss roll

Fresh summer fruits such as strawberries, peaches and nectarines have a natural affinity with cream. Here, these aromatic fruits are combined with whipping cream, which has a lower fat content than double cream, plus a little Greek-style yogurt to make a delicious filling for a light-as-air fatless sponge.

Serves 8

3 large eggs

115 g (4 oz) caster sugar

115 g (4 oz) plain flour

1 tbsp tepid water

Summer fruit filling

150 ml (5 fl oz) whipping cream

1 tsp pure vanilla extract

75 g (2½ oz) Greek-style yogurt

125 g (4½ oz) small strawberries, sliced

1 ripe peach or nectarine, chopped

To decorate

2–3 tbsp icing sugar, sifted

a few slices of strawberry and peach or
    nectarine

Preparation time: 30 minutes

Cooking time: 10–12 minutes

1 Preheat the oven to 200°C (400°F, gas mark 6). Grease a 33 x 23 cm (13 x 9 in) Swiss roll tin and line with baking parchment.

2 Put the eggs and sugar in a large bowl and beat with an electric mixer until the mixture is very thick and pale, and leaves a trail on the surface when the beaters are lifted out. (If using a hand whisk or rotary beater, set the bowl over a pan of almost boiling water, making sure the water is not touching the base of the bowl.)

3 Sift half the flour over the whisked mixture and gently fold it in with a large metal spoon. Sift over the remaining flour and fold in together with the tepid water.

4 Pour the mixture into the prepared tin and give it a gentle shake so that the mixture spreads evenly into the corners. Bake for 10–12 minutes or until the sponge is well risen and pale golden, and springs back when pressed gently with your finger.

5 Turn out onto a sheet of baking parchment slightly larger than the sponge. Peel off the lining paper. Trim the crusty edges of the sponge with a sharp knife and make a score mark 2.5 cm (1 in) from one of the shorter edges (this will make the sponge easier to roll up).

6 Roll up loosely from the short side, with the paper inside, and place seam side down on a wire rack to cool.

7 When the sponge is cold, carefully unroll it and remove the paper. Whip the cream with the vanilla extract until it forms soft peaks, then fold in the yogurt. Spread this mixture over the sponge, leaving a 1 cm (½ in) border all round. Scatter the fruit over the cream. Carefully roll up the sponge and place seam side down on a serving plate.

8 Lay 2 cm (¾ in) strips of kitchen paper or greaseproof paper diagonally, at an equal distance apart, over the sponge roll, then dust with the icing sugar. Carefully remove the paper, to leave a striped effect. Decorate with the extra fruit. Keep the roll in the fridge until ready to serve. This classic fatless sponge does not keep well and is best eaten within a day of making.

Plus points

- Strawberries are an excellent source of vitamin C – weight for weight they contain more than oranges. They also provide useful amounts of fibre and folate.
- Peaches are another rich source of vitamin C and of vitamin A (from beta-carotene).

Each serving provides Ⓥ

kcal 240, **protein** 5 g, **fat** 11 g (of which saturated fat 6 g), **carbohydrate** 33 g (of which sugars 22 g), **fibre** 1 g

✓✓	A, B$_{12}$, C
✓	B$_2$

Some more ideas

• For a simple jam Swiss roll, follow the main recipe to the end of step 5, then spread the sponge with 5 tbsp warmed jam and roll up. Sprinkle with 2 tsp caster sugar. Serve with fromage frais, if liked.

• For a chocolate and raspberry Swiss roll, replace 3 tbsp of the flour with 3 tbsp cocoa powder. Use 170 g (6 oz) fresh raspberries in the filling instead of strawberries and peaches. Decorate with icing sugar and cocoa powder.

• For a coffee sponge cake, pour 1½ tbsp almost boiling water over 2 tsp ground coffee, leave to infuse for 4 minutes and then strain. Fold the liquid into the sponge mixture instead of the tepid water. Divide the mixture equally between 2 greased and bottom-lined 18 cm (7 in) sandwich tins, then bake at 190°C (375°F, gas mark 5) for 20–25 minutes. Turn out and cool on a wire rack. Sandwich together with 5 tbsp warmed apricot jam.

• For an orange sponge cake, whisk the finely grated zest of 1 orange with the sugar and eggs. Bake in sandwich tins as above.

31

Banana cake

Quick and easy to prepare using storecupboard ingredients, this cut-and-come-again cake makes a healthy snack for hungry children just back from school, or a handy addition to lunchboxes. It's best made with very ripe bananas, so it's a good way of using up bananas that have been sitting in the fruit bowl for too long.

Serves 8

2 large, ripe bananas, about 400 g (14 oz) in total, weighed with their skins on
250 g (8½ oz) self-raising flour
1 tsp baking powder
50 g (1¾ oz) light muscovado sugar
6 tbsp sunflower oil
6 tbsp semi-skimmed milk
2 eggs
115 g (4 oz) sultanas

Preparation time: 10 minutes
Cooking time: 50–55 minutes

1 Preheat the oven to 180ºC (350ºF, gas mark 4). Grease an 18 cm (7 in) round deep cake tin and line the bottom with baking parchment. Peel the bananas, then mash with a fork.

2 Sift the flour and baking powder into a bowl and stir in the sugar. Whisk together the oil, milk and eggs and add to the flour mixture. Stir in the sultanas and mashed bananas, then pour the mixture into the prepared tin.

3 Bake for 50–55 minutes or until the cake is well risen and a skewer inserted in the centre comes out clean. Leave to cool for 15 minutes, then loosen the edge of the cake with a knife and turn it out onto a wire rack to cool completely. The cake can be kept in an airtight tin for up to 4 days.

Some more ideas

● Substitute other fruit for the sultanas, such as dried cranberries, chopped dried figs or ready-to-eat dried apricots, or a mix of chopped ready-to-eat exotic dried fruits.

● Decorate the top of the cake with glacé icing. Mix 100 g (3½ oz) sifted icing sugar with about 1 tbsp fresh orange juice, and drizzle in random lines from the tip of a spoon or using a greaseproof paper icing bag.

● To make banana and pecan muffins, substitute 100 g (3½ oz) roughly chopped pecan nuts for the sultanas and add 6 tbsp plain low-fat bio yogurt with the oil, milk and eggs. Divide among a 12-cup deep muffin tin lined with paper muffin cases. Bake at 200ºC (400ºF, gas mark 6) for about 20 minutes or until well risen and golden.

Plus points

● This cake is much lower in sugar than a conventional banana cake. Using sunflower oil instead of butter makes it low in saturated fat too.

● Bananas are a great energy booster and rich in potassium, vital for muscle and nerve function and to help regulate blood pressure.

Each serving provides Ⓥ

kcal 310, **protein** 6 g, **fat** 10 g (of which saturated fat 2 g), **carbohydrate** 50 g (of which sugars 26 g), **fibre** 2 g

✓✓ B_6, B_{12}

✓ B_1, calcium, copper, iron

cakes for all occasions

Gingerbread

This delicious dark, lightly spiced gingerbread is hard to resist. Enjoy a slice with a cup of tea or try it for pudding, with custard or a little cream or crème fraîche plus, perhaps, a spoonful of fresh apple compote.

Serves 10

115 g (4 oz) light muscovado sugar
85 g (3 oz) unsalted butter
170 g (6 oz) molasses
85 g (3 oz) plain white flour
85 g (3 oz) plain wholemeal flour
55 g (2 oz) rye flour
1 tsp bicarbonate of soda
pinch of salt
1 tbsp ground ginger
1 tsp ground mixed spice
2 eggs
150 ml (5 fl oz) semi-skimmed milk

Preparation time: 20 minutes
Cooking time: 1¼–1½ hours

Each serving provides

kcal 240, **protein** 4 g, **fat** 7 g (of which saturated fat 4 g), **carbohydrate** 41 g (of which sugars 23 g), **fibre** 2 g

✓ A, B$_6$, B$_{12}$, calcium, copper, iron, selenium, zinc

1 Preheat the oven to 160°C (325°F, gas mark 3). Lightly grease a 900 g (2 lb) loaf tin and line the bottom with baking parchment.

2 Place the sugar, butter and molasses in a saucepan and heat gently until melted and well blended, stirring occasionally. Remove from the heat and cool slightly.

3 Sift the white flour, wholemeal flour, rye flour, bicarbonate of soda, salt, ginger and mixed spice into a large bowl, tipping in any bran left in the sieve. Make a well in the centre and pour in the melted mixture, together with the eggs and milk. Beat together until smooth (the mixture will be very runny). Pour into the prepared tin.

4 Bake for 1¼–1½ hours or until risen, firm to the touch and nicely browned. Leave the cake to cool in the tin for a few minutes, then turn it out onto a wire rack to cool completely. Gingerbread can be kept, wrapped in foil or in an airtight container, for up to 1 week.

Some more ideas

● Use half molasses and half golden syrup for a slightly lighter gingerbread.
● Make moist apple gingerbread, which is lower in sugar and fat than the main recipe. Peel, core and thinly slice 1 dessert apple (about 140 g/5 oz) and place it in a small pan with 1 tbsp water. Cover and cook gently for 10–15 minutes or until soft and pulpy, stirring occasionally. Remove from the heat and mash the apple to a purée, then set aside to cool. Make the cake mixture as in the main recipe, but reducing the sugar to 55 g (2 oz) and the butter to 45 g (1½ oz). Add the apple purée with the melted mixture.

Plus points

● Molasses is the syrup left over after sugar has been crystallised from the juice of the sugar cane. It is a concentrated source of several minerals, including magnesium, copper, iron, calcium and potassium, although it is rarely eaten in large enough quantities to contribute significant amounts of these nutrients to the diet.
● Compared with wheat flour, rye flour has very little gluten, which explains why rye breads such as pumpernickel tend to have a heavier texture. Rye flour contains high quantities of pentosans (long-chain sugars), which have a high water-binding capacity. Baked goods made with rye flour retain moisture, which means they swell in the stomach, giving the sensation of fullness.

Frosted chocolate ring cake

Chocolate cake is always popular. This updated version is enriched with a sweet prune purée and topped with a creamy Italian-style frosting. Serve it at tea-time or for dessert – perfect with some fresh berries on the side.

Serves 10

140 g (5 oz) stoned ready-to-eat prunes

150 ml (5 fl oz) boiling water

55 g (2 oz) unsalted butter, at room temperature

140 g (5 oz) light muscovado sugar

1 tsp pure vanilla extract

2 eggs, beaten

100 g (3½ oz) self-raising white flour

100 g (3½ oz) self-raising wholemeal flour

1 tsp baking powder

4 tbsp cocoa powder, plus extra to dust

Ricotta frosting

250 g (8½ oz) ricotta cheese

½ tsp pure vanilla extract

1 tbsp icing sugar, or to taste, sifted

Preparation time: 25 minutes, plus 30 minutes soaking

Cooking time: 25 minutes

Each serving provides Ⓥ

kcal 250, **protein** 7 g, **fat** 9 g (of which saturated fat 5 g), **carbohydrate** 36 g (of which sugars 22 g), **fibre** 2 g

✓   A, B₁, B₂, B₆, B₁₂, calcium, copper, iron, selenium, zinc

1 Place the prunes in a bowl and pour over the boiling water. Cover and set aside to soak for 30 minutes.

2 Preheat the oven to 180°C (350°F, gas mark 4). Grease a 20 cm (8 in) ring tin, 900 ml (1½ pints) in capacity.

3 Beat the butter until soft and light, then gradually beat in the sugar. Purée the prunes with their soaking liquid in a blender until smooth, then add to the butter and sugar mixture with the vanilla extract, beating until well mixed. Gradually beat in the eggs.

4 Sift the white flour, wholemeal flour, baking powder and cocoa powder over the mixture, tipping in any bran left in the sieve. Fold in the dry ingredients until evenly combined in a mixture that has a soft dropping consistency, adding a little water if necessary. Transfer it to the ring tin and spread it out evenly.

5 Bake for about 25 minutes or until well risen, slightly cracked on top and firm to the touch. Leave in the tin for 10 minutes, then run a knife around the inside of the tin to loosen the cake and turn it out onto a wire rack to cool. (The cake can be kept in an airtight tin for 3 days, before adding the topping.)

6 To make the frosting, press the ricotta through a sieve into a bowl. Add the vanilla extract and icing sugar, and beat until smooth.

7 Place the cake on a serving plate and spoon the ricotta frosting evenly around the top. Use a knife to swirl the frosting slightly, taking it a short way down the side of the cake. Place a little cocoa powder in a tea strainer or small sieve and dust it over the frosting. Serve as soon as possible.

Some more ideas

● Add 100 g (3½ oz) finely chopped walnuts to the mixture after sifting in the flour. Decorate the frosting with a few walnut halves.

● For a fruit-filled ring cake, slice the ring into 2 layers and sandwich them together with half the ricotta frosting and 100 g (3½ oz) sliced strawberries or whole blueberries. Top the cake with the remaining frosting and decorate with a few whole strawberries or blueberries.

Plus points

● Prunes have a lot to offer nutritionally, being a good source of fibre, as well as providing several vitamins, minerals and phytochemicals. Made into a purée, they can replace some of the fat and sugar in baked goods (see also page 19).

● Ricotta is relatively low in fat (11 g fat per 100 g/3½ oz compared with cream cheese at 47 g fat), and is a good source of protein, calcium and vitamins B₂ and B₁₂.

cakes for all occasions

Date and walnut cake

This old-fashioned favourite is proof that you don't need to invent new recipes in order to eat healthily. Despite being very low in fat it has a lovely light, moist texture, thanks to the dried dates, and makes a pleasant alternative to a conventional fruited cake. It's delightfully easy to make, and keeps well too.

Serves 10

200 g (7 oz) stoned dried dates, chopped
30 g (1 oz) unsalted butter
1 tsp bicarbonate of soda
240 ml (8 fl oz) boiling water
140 g (5 oz) light muscovado sugar
2 eggs
280 g (10 oz) plain flour
2 tsp baking powder
1½ tsp ground mixed spice
pinch of salt
115 g (4 oz) walnuts, chopped

Preparation time: 20 minutes, plus soaking
Cooking time: 1–1¼ hours

1 Place the dates in a bowl with the butter and bicarbonate of soda. Pour over the boiling water and stir until the butter has melted. Set aside to cool.

2 Preheat the oven to 180°C (350°F, gas mark 4). Lightly grease an 18 cm (7 in) round deep cake tin and line the bottom with baking parchment.

3 Place the sugar and eggs in a large bowl and beat well to combine. Add the cooled date mixture, then sift in the flour, baking powder, mixed spice and salt. Add the walnuts and stir together until thoroughly mixed.

4 Pour the mixture into the prepared tin and level the top. Bake for 1–1¼ hours or until the cake is risen and nicely browned and a skewer inserted in the centre comes out clean.

5 Turn out onto a wire rack and leave to cool. The cake can be kept, wrapped in foil or stored in an airtight container, for up to 5 days.

Some more ideas

● Replace the walnuts with other nuts, such as pecans or hazelnuts.
● Replace some or all of the dates with chopped ready-to-eat prunes or dried figs.
● Use half white and half wholemeal flour instead of all white flour.
● Drizzle the cooled cake with lemon glacé icing, made by mixing 100 g (3½ oz) sifted icing sugar with 1 tbsp fresh lemon juice.

Plus points

● Walnuts are high in unsaturated fats, especially linoleic acid, and recent studies have shown that people who eat walnuts regularly are less likely to suffer from heart attacks. Walnuts are rich in protein, vitamin E, vitamin B_6 and copper, and provide useful amounts of vitamin B_1 and selenium. In traditional Chinese medicine walnuts are used to treat impotency.
● Dates were one of the first fruits to be cultivated by man. Remains of the date palm have been discovered during archaeological excavation of several Stone Age sites. Dried dates are a good source of potassium and provide useful amounts of niacin, copper, iron and magnesium.

Each serving provides

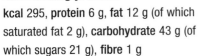

kcal 295, **protein** 6 g, **fat** 12 g (of which saturated fat 2 g), **carbohydrate** 43 g (of which sugars 21 g), **fibre** 1 g

✓ B_1, B_6, B_{12}, calcium, copper, zinc

cakes for all occasions

39

Spanish orange and almond cake

Made with whole oranges – simmered until very tender and then finely chopped – and ground almonds, this classic Spanish cake has a moist, light texture and a wonderful fresh flavour.

Serves 10

2 oranges, about 280 g (10 oz) in total, scrubbed and roughly chopped (with skin)

5 eggs, separated

200 g (7 oz) caster sugar

225 g (8 oz) ground almonds

2 tbsp flaked almonds

sifted icing sugar to decorate

Preparation time: 1 hour
Cooking time: 50–55 minutes

Each serving provides (V)

kcal 290, **protein** 9 g, **fat** 17 g (of which saturated fat 2 g), **carbohydrate** 25 g (of which sugars 25 g), **fibre** 2 g

✓✓	B₁₂, C
✓	A, B₁, B₂, folate, calcium, copper, zinc

1 Put the chopped oranges in a small saucepan, discarding any pips. Add 1 tbsp water, then cover and cook gently for 30 minutes or until the oranges are soft and excess liquid has evaporated. Leave to cool.

2 Preheat the oven to 180°C (350°F, gas mark 4). Line the bottom and sides of a 23 cm (9 in) springform cake tin with baking parchment. Finely chop the oranges in a food processor or blender, or with a large knife.

3 Put the egg whites in a large bowl and whisk until they form stiff peaks. Gradually whisk in half the caster sugar, then whisk for 1 minute.

4 Using the same whisk, whisk the egg yolks with the remaining caster sugar in another bowl for 2–3 minutes or until pale and quite thick. Whisk in the finely chopped oranges, then carefully fold in the ground almonds.

5 Stir in 3 spoonfuls of the whisked egg white to loosen the mixture, then gently fold in the remaining whites with a large metal spoon. Transfer the mixture to the prepared tin and level the top. Sprinkle with the flaked almonds.

6 Bake for 50–55 minutes or until the cake is golden and a skewer inserted in the centre comes out clean. Check the cake after 20 minutes and again at 30 minutes, and cover lightly with foil if it is browning too quickly.

7 Leave the cake to cool in the tin, then turn it out, peel away the lining paper and transfer to a serving plate. Dust with icing sugar before serving. The cake can be kept in an airtight tin for up to 2 days.

Some more ideas

• Instead of ground almonds alone, use a mixture of 100 g (3½ oz) each ground almonds and semolina or instant polenta. This cake will be a little drier, so drizzle 2–3 tbsp Grand Marnier, Amaretto liqueur, tequila or orange juice over it rather than dusting with icing sugar. It is delicious served with a mixture of 150 ml (5 fl oz) whipped whipping cream and 150 g (5½ oz) fromage frais.

• For a St Clement's cake, substitute a lemon for one of the oranges, and decorate the top with thin strips of candied citrus peel instead of the flaked almonds.

Plus points

• Using whole oranges boosts the fibre and vitamin C content of this cake. Studies have shown a connection between a regular intake of vitamin C and the maintenance of intellectual function in elderly people.

• As the cake is made without flour, it is suitable for those on gluten-free or wheat-free diets.

Rich fruit ring cake

Most rich fruit cakes are high in fat and added sugar, but this one is an exception. It's relatively low in fat, and depends mainly on dried fruits soaked in apple juice for natural sweetness. Decorated with nuts, and glacé and crystallised fruits, it makes a healthy cake that would be festive enough for Christmas!

Serves 18

85 g (3 oz) dried cranberries
85 g (3 oz) sultanas
85 g (3 oz) dried pears, chopped
85 g (3 oz) stoned prunes, chopped
85 g (3 oz) dried figs, chopped
85 g (3 oz) stoned dried dates, chopped
250 ml (8½ fl oz) apple juice
50 g (1¾ oz) pecan nuts, chopped
50 g (1¾ oz) candied ginger, chopped
finely grated zest and juice of 1 lemon
5 tbsp sunflower oil
1 egg
75 g (2½ oz) molasses sugar
115 g (4 oz) self-raising white flour
115 g (4 oz) self-raising wholemeal flour
1 tsp baking powder
2 tsp ground mixed spice
3–4 tbsp semi-skimmed milk, as needed

Decoration

2 tbsp apricot jam
55 g (2 oz) glacé cherries
30 g (1 oz) hazelnuts
40 g (1¼ oz) pecan nut halves
40 g (1¼ oz) walnut halves
55 g (2 oz) candied ginger, sliced
icing sugar to dust

Preparation time: about 30 minutes, plus
    soaking and 2–3 weeks maturing
Cooking time: 1¼–1½ hours

1 Place all the dried fruit in a medium-sized saucepan. Add the apple juice, place over a moderate heat and bring slowly to the boil. Cover and simmer gently for 3–4 minutes or until the fruit begins to absorb the liquid.

2 Remove the pan from the heat and leave, covered, until completely cold. Stir in the pecan nuts, ginger, and lemon zest and juice.

3 Preheat the oven to 150°C (300°F, gas mark 2). Brush a 23 cm (9 in) ring tin with a little oil. In a bowl, beat together the sunflower oil, egg and sugar until smooth.

4 Sift the white and wholemeal flours, baking powder and mixed spice into a large bowl, tipping in any bran left in the sieve. Add the soaked fruit and the egg mixture, and stir well to combine thoroughly. Stir in enough milk to make a fairly soft mixture.

5 Spoon the mixture into the prepared tin and smooth the top. Bake for 1¼–1½ hours or until risen, firm and golden brown, and just beginning to shrink away from the sides of the tin.

6 Leave the cake to cool in the tin for at least 1 hour before running a knife around the edge and turning it out. Wrap in greaseproof paper and foil, and store for 2–3 weeks before serving, to allow the flavours to mature.

7 To decorate the cake, gently heat the jam with 1 tsp water, then press through a sieve. Brush the top of the cake with the jam. Arrange the cherries, nuts and candied ginger on top, pressing them gently into the jam. Finally, dust with sifted icing sugar.

Some more ideas

● For easier slicing, bake the cake in a long loaf tin, about 1.4 litres (2½ pints) in capacity.
● Soak the fruit in cherry brandy instead of apple juice.

Plus points

● Dried figs are a good source of fibre and also contain compounds known to have mild laxative effects. Drying the fruit concentrates their nutrients, making them a useful source of calcium and iron.
● Pecans are a good source of protein and unsaturated fats, and they provide useful amounts of vitamin E, folate and fibre.

Each serving provides Ⓥ
kcal 250, **protein** 4 g, **fat** 10 g (of which saturated fat 1 g), **carbohydrate** 38 g (of which sugars 29 g), **fibre** 3 g

✓ B₆, copper

Carrot and brazil nut cake

Scrumptious American-style carrot cake is a great way to get children to eat vegetables without even noticing. The creamy icing here is lighter in fat than a traditional one, as it uses ricotta cheese.

Serves 10

170 g (6 oz) self-raising wholemeal flour
170 g (6 oz) self-raising white flour
1 tsp ground cinnamon
100 g (3½ oz) brazil nuts
55 g (2 oz) raisins
140 g (5 oz) light muscovado sugar
200 ml (7 fl oz) sunflower oil
4 large eggs
200 g (7 oz) carrots (about 3 carrots), finely grated
finely grated zest and juice of ½ orange

Orange ricotta icing

250 g (8½ oz) ricotta cheese
55 g (2 oz) icing sugar, sifted
finely grated zest of ½ orange

Preparation time: 30 minutes
Cooking time: 50 minutes

Each serving provides Ⓥ

kcal 480, **protein** 10 g, **fat** 27 g (of which saturated fat 6 g), **carbohydrate** 51 g (of which sugars 27 g), **fibre** 3 g

✓✓✓	A, E, selenium
✓✓	B₁, B₁₂, copper, zinc
✓	B₂, B₆, folate, calcium, iron

1 Preheat the oven to 180°C (350°F, gas mark 4). Grease a 20 cm (8 in) round deep cake tin and line the bottom with baking parchment.

2 Sift the wholemeal and white flours and the cinnamon into a large bowl, tipping in any bran left in the sieve. Coarsely chop about two-thirds of the brazil nuts and stir into the flour with the raisins. Thinly slice the rest of the brazil nuts lengthways and set aside.

3 In another bowl, beat together the sugar and oil with a wooden spoon until well combined. Beat in the eggs one at a time, then stir in the grated carrots and orange zest and juice. With a large metal spoon, carefully fold the carrot mixture into the flour mixture, just until combined. Do not overmix.

4 Spoon the mixture into the prepared tin. Bake for 50 minutes or until risen and firm to the touch. Leave the cake in the tin for 5 minutes, then turn out onto a wire rack and peel off the lining paper. Cool completely.

5 To make the icing, put the ricotta in a bowl, add the sugar and orange zest, and beat with a wooden spoon.

6 When the cake is cold, spread the icing on top. Scatter over the reserved sliced brazil nuts, letting some stick up out of the icing at different angles. The cake can be kept, covered, in the fridge for up to 3 days.

Some more ideas

• Substitute cashew or macadamia nuts for the brazils.
• Use quark instead of ricotta to make the icing. For a honey icing, mix the ricotta or quark with 1 tbsp each clear honey and icing sugar.
• To make a passion cake, drain a can of pineapple in natural juice, about 227 g, and chop finely. Pat the pineapple between several sheets of kitchen paper to absorb excess moisture. Use 150 g (5½ oz) grated carrots, and stir in the pineapple with the carrots. Omit the orange juice, and use pecan nuts instead of brazil nuts.

Plus points

• Wholemeal flour is a useful source of many of the B vitamins, plus iron and zinc. It also provides good amounts of fibre, particularly the insoluble variety.
• Carrots are one of the richest sources of the antioxidant beta-carotene, which helps to protect cells against damage by free radicals. Most vegetables are more nutritious eaten raw, but carrots have more to offer when cooked. This is because cooking breaks down the tough cell membranes in the carrots, and makes it easier for the body to absorb the beta-carotene.

Strawberry shortcake

This streamlined version of an American classic makes an impressive summer dessert or centrepiece for a special tea table. Based on a quick, light scone mixture and filled with Greek-style yogurt, whipped cream and lots of juicy fresh strawberries, it is easy to make and simply irresistible.

Serves 8

250 g (8½ oz) self-raising flour

1 tsp baking powder

75 g (2½ oz) unsalted butter, cut into small pieces

3 tbsp caster sugar

1 egg, beaten

4 tbsp semi-skimmed milk

½ tsp pure vanilla extract

1 tsp icing sugar

Strawberry filling

340 g (12 oz) strawberries

90 ml (3 fl oz) whipping cream

85 g (3 oz) Greek-style yogurt

Preparation time: 15 minutes

Cooking time: 10–15 minutes

1 Preheat the oven to 220°C (425°F, gas mark 7). Sift the flour and baking powder into a bowl. Rub in the butter with your fingertips until the mixture resembles fine breadcrumbs. Stir in the caster sugar and make a well in the centre.

2 Mix together the egg, milk and vanilla extract, and pour into the dry ingredients. Gradually stir the dry ingredients into the liquid, then bring the mixture together with your hand to form a soft dough. Gently pat the dough into a smooth ball and turn it out onto a floured surface.

3 Roll out the dough into a 19 cm (7½ in) round. Transfer it to a greased baking sheet and bake for 10–15 minutes or until well risen, firm and browned on top. Slide the shortcake onto a wire rack and leave to cool.

4 Using a large serrated knife, slice the shortcake horizontally in half. With a large fish slice, lift the top layer off and place it on a board. Cut into 8 equal wedges, leaving them in place. (If you like, for an attractive finish, trim a fraction off each cut so that the wedges are slightly smaller.) Place the bottom layer on a serving plate.

5 For the filling, reserve 8 whole strawberries, then hull and thickly slice the remainder. Whip the cream

until it forms soft peaks. Stir the yogurt until smooth, then gently fold it into the cream until evenly blended.

6 Spread the cream mixture thickly over the bottom shortcake layer and cover with the sliced strawberries, pressing them into the cream.

7 Sift the icing sugar over the top of the shortcake wedges. Carefully put the wedges into place on top of the shortcake. Slice each reserved strawberry lengthways, leaving the slices attached at the stalk end, then open the slices slightly to fan them out. Place a strawberry fan on each wedge of shortcake. Eat within a few hours of assembling.

Each serving provides Ⓥ

kcal 275, **protein** 5 g, **fat** 14 g (of which saturated fat 8 g), **carbohydrate** 34 g (of which sugars 10 g), **fibre** 1 g

✓✓✓	C
✓✓	A
✓	B₁, B₂, B₆, B₁₂, calcium

Plus points

• Strawberries contain a phytochemical called ellagic acid, which is believed to help protect against cancer. In traditional medicine, strawberries are believed to purify the digestive system and act as a mild tonic for the liver.

• The action of whipping incorporates air into cream and increases its volume, thus making a modest amount go a long way.

Some more ideas

• Raspberries, blueberries and stoned cherries can all be substituted for the strawberries.

• To make a spiced shortcake with autumn fruit, add 1 tsp ground cinnamon to the scone mixture with the caster sugar. Halve, stone and slice 225 g (8 oz) ripe plums. Reserve 8 neat slices for decoration, then use the rest to top the cream in place of the strawberries. Reserve 8 blackberries from 225 g (8 oz) and press the remainder into the cream with the plums. Finish as in the main recipe, decorating the top of the shortcake wedges with the reserved plum slices and blackberries.

• Instead of whipped cream and yogurt, fill the shortcake with 300 g (10½ oz) fromage frais flavoured with 2 tsp icing sugar and ½ tsp pure vanilla extract.

Glazed mango sponge

In this unusual upside-down cake, juicy slices of mango are topped with a simple, light sponge mixture flavoured with lime zest and coconut. After baking, the cake is turned out so that the fruit is on top, then dredged with icing sugar and caramelised to a golden brown under a hot grill.

Serves 8

1 ripe mango
170 g (6 oz) caster sugar
2 eggs, lightly beaten
115 g (4 oz) plain low-fat yogurt
120 ml (4 fl oz) sunflower oil
finely grated zest of 1 lime
170 g (6 oz) plain flour
1½ tsp baking powder
30 g (1 oz) desiccated coconut
2 tbsp icing sugar, sifted

Preparation time: 20 minutes
Cooking time: 50 minutes

Each serving provides Ⓥ
kcal 335, **protein** 5 g, **fat** 15 g (of which saturated fat 4 g), **carbohydrate** 48 g (of which sugars 31 g), **fibre** 2 g

✓✓✓ E

✓ A, B₆, B₁₂, C, calcium

1 Preheat the oven to 180°C (350°F, gas mark 4). Grease a loose-bottomed 18 cm (7 in) square deep cake tin, or a 20 cm (8 in) round deep cake tin, and line the bottom with baking parchment.

2 Peel the mango. Cut the flesh away from the stone and cut it into thin slices. Arrange over the bottom of the prepared cake tin.

3 Put the caster sugar, eggs, yogurt, oil and lime zest into a large bowl and stir until smooth and well mixed. Sift over the flour and baking powder and fold in, together with the coconut.

4 Spoon the mixture into the tin, over the sliced mango, and level the top. Bake for 50 minutes or until golden brown and firm to the touch, covering with foil after 30 minutes if the cake begins to brown too much.

5 Leave the cake in the tin for about 15 minutes, then turn out onto the rack of a grill pan, mango-side up, and peel off the lining paper. Thickly dust with the icing sugar and place under a preheated hot grill for 3–4 minutes or until the sugar has melted and is golden. Leave to cool on the rack.

6 Transfer the cake to a plate for serving. Any leftover cake can be covered with cling film and kept in the fridge for 2–3 days.

Plus points

- Sunflower oil is rich in polyunsaturated fats and vitamin E, a powerful antioxidant that helps to protect cell membranes against damage from free radicals. Sunflower oil should be stored in a cool, dark place because the vitamin E is destroyed by exposure to sunlight.

- Mangoes are rich in several carotenoid compounds, including beta-carotene and vitamin C. They are a good source of potassium, a key mineral for people with high blood pressure. They also contain a phytochemical called beta cryptoxanthin. Studies have shown that women who have high levels of this compound in their blood are less at risk of developing cervical cancer.

Some more ideas

● For a chocolate, pear and walnut upside-down cake, use 2 ripe but firm pears, peeled, cored and sliced, instead of the mango. Substitute 3 tbsp cocoa powder for 3 tbsp of the plain flour, and fold in 30 g (1 oz) finely chopped walnuts instead of the coconut.

● For a peach and almond sponge, put 115 g (4 oz) softened unsalted butter, 115 g (4 oz) light muscovado sugar, 45 g (1½ oz) plain wholemeal flour, 45 g (1½ oz) self-raising white flour, 1 tsp baking powder, 30 g (1 oz) ground almonds, 2 eggs and 1 tbsp milk in a large bowl. Beat well for about 2 minutes or until blended. Spoon the mixture into a greased and lined 23 cm (9 in) springform cake tin. Halve and stone 3 ripe but firm peaches. Turn the peach halves rounded side up and slice each one into 6–7 wedges, not cutting all the way through. Arrange, sliced side up, on top of the sponge. Bake as in the main recipe.

Italian rice cake with red fruit

Here's an unusual flourless cake that makes a delightful dessert. Italian risotto rice is cooked slowly in milk until tender and creamy, then mixed with eggs, nuts, lemon and rum, and baked. It's served with a red fruit salad.

Serves 8
600 ml (1 pint) semi-skimmed milk
a strip of lemon zest
150 g (5½ oz) risotto rice
100 g (3½ oz) pine nuts
100 g (3½ oz) blanched almonds
3 large eggs, separated
85 g (3 oz) caster sugar
grated zest of 1 lemon
1 tbsp dark rum
sifted icing sugar to decorate
Red fruit salad
300 g (10½ oz) strawberries
125 g (4½ oz) raspberries
200 g (7 oz) cherries, stoned

Preparation time: 1¼ hours, plus chilling
    overnight
Cooking time: 40 minutes

Each serving provides ⓥ
kcal 365, **protein** 12 g, **fat** 19 g (of which
saturated fat 2 g), **carbohydrate** 37 g (of
which sugars 21 g), **fibre** 2 g

✓✓✓	C, E
✓✓	B₂, B₁₂, copper, zinc
✓	A, B₁, folate, calcium, iron, potassium

1 Heat the milk with the strip of lemon zest in a heavy-based saucepan until boiling. Stir in the rice, then turn down the heat so the milk barely simmers. Cook uncovered, stirring frequently, for about 40 minutes or until the rice is very soft and the mixture is thick and creamy.

2 Spoon the rice mixture into a large bowl and leave to cool. Meanwhile, preheat the oven to 180°C (350°F, gas mark 4). Grease a 21 cm (8½ in) springform cake tin and line the bottom with baking parchment.

3 Spread the pine nuts and almonds in separate baking tins and toast in the oven for 10 minutes or until lightly browned. Roughly chop the almonds.

4 Remove the strip of lemon zest from the rice. Using a wooden spoon, beat in the egg yolks one at a time. Beat in the caster sugar, grated lemon zest and rum, then add the nuts.

5 In a separate bowl, whisk the egg whites until they form stiff peaks. Gently fold them into the rice mixture using a large metal spoon. Spoon the mixture into the prepared tin and bake for about 40 minutes or until a skewer inserted in the centre comes out clean.

6 Leave the cake to cool in the tin, then wrap (still in the tin) and chill overnight. (It can be kept in the fridge for 48 hours, if necessary.)

7 To make the red fruit salad, purée 100 g (3½ oz) of the strawberries in a food processor or blender, or by pushing them through a sieve. Halve the remaining strawberries and stir into the purée together with the raspberries and cherries. Spoon into a serving bowl.

8 Unmould the cake onto a serving plate and peel off the lining paper. Dust the cake with icing sugar, and serve with the fruit salad.

Another idea
• To make a chocolate rice cake, cook the rice with the strip of lemon zest as in the main recipe, then remove from the heat and discard the lemon zest. While the rice mixture is still hot, stir in 55 g (2 oz) grated good dark chocolate (with at least 70% cocoa solids) until melted, then leave to cool. Instead of the grated lemon zest, add 2 tbsp cold strong espresso coffee with the rum.

Plus points
• Pine nuts have been eaten for hundreds of years – husks have been found in the rubbish tips from Roman camps in Britain. Pine nuts contain useful amounts of iron, magnesium, zinc, potassium and vitamin E.
• Cherries are rich in potassium, and provide useful amounts of vitamin C.

cakes for all occasions

Hazelnut meringue cake

Simply add long wand candles to turn this light but gooey meringue into a birthday cake. As it has a pastry cream and fresh raspberry filling, it's much lower in fat and calories than conventional celebration cakes.

Serves 6

65 g (2¼ oz) hazelnuts

4 egg whites

225 g (8 oz) caster sugar

225 g (8 oz) fresh raspberries

sifted icing sugar to decorate

Vanilla pastry cream

300 ml (10 fl oz) semi-skimmed milk, plus
  2 tbsp extra if needed

1 vanilla pod, slit open lengthways

3 egg yolks

30 g (1 oz) caster sugar

15 g (½ oz) plain flour

15 g (½ oz) cornflour

Preparation time: 40 minutes, plus 30 minutes
  standing

Cooking time: 1¼ hours

Each serving provides   ⓥ

kcal 330, **protein** 8 g, **fat** 10 g (of which
saturated fat 2 g), **carbohydrate** 53 g (of
which sugars 49 g), **fibre** 2 g

✓✓ B₁₂, C, E

✓ A, B₁, B₂, B₆, folate, calcium, copper,
  zinc

---

1 Preheat the grill, then toast the hazelnuts until golden. Leave to cool. Roughly chop a few for the decoration and set aside; finely chop or grind the rest of the hazelnuts in a nut mill or food processor.

2 Preheat the oven to 140°C (275°F, gas mark 1). Line 2 baking sheets with baking parchment and draw a 20 cm (8 in) circle on each piece of parchment.

3 Whisk the egg whites in a large bowl until they form stiff peaks. Gradually whisk in the caster sugar a tablespoon at a time, then continue to whisk for 1–2 minutes or until the meringue is very thick and glossy. Fold in the finely chopped or ground hazelnuts with a large metal spoon.

4 Divide the meringue between the baking sheets and spread evenly within the drawn circles. Bake for 1¼ hours or until the meringues are set and can be easily removed from the paper; switch round the baking sheets halfway through cooking so that the meringues colour evenly. Loosen the meringues from the paper, then leave to cool completely on the baking sheets.

5 To make the pastry cream, pour the milk into a saucepan and bring to the boil. Add the vanilla pod, then remove from the heat and leave to infuse for 30 minutes.

6 Whisk the egg yolks with the sugar for 2–3 minutes or until pale. Sift in the flour and cornflour, and whisk to combine. Remove the vanilla pod from the milk and scrape the seeds into the milk with a sharp knife; discard the pod. Bring the milk just to the boil, then gradually whisk it into the egg yolk mixture.

7 Pour the mixture back into the saucepan and bring to the boil, stirring constantly with a wooden spoon or a whisk. When thick, simmer gently for 1 minute, still stirring constantly. Remove from the heat. Cover the surface of the pastry cream with wet greaseproof paper and leave to cool. (Both the meringues and pastry cream can be made a day in advance; store the meringues in an airtight container and the pastry cream in a covered bowl in the fridge.)

8 Assemble the cake no more than 1 hour before serving. Place one of the meringues on a serving plate, flat side uppermost, and spread over the pastry cream (if it is too thick to spread, beat in the extra milk). Sprinkle with two-thirds of the raspberries, then top with the second meringue. Decorate with the remaining raspberries, roughly chopped toasted hazelnuts and a light dusting of icing sugar. Cut into thick slices with a sharp knife to serve.

Plus points

- Eggs are a good source of protein and provide useful amounts of vitamins A, B_2, B_{12}, E, folate, selenium and phosphorus.
- Raspberries are an excellent source of vitamin C and a useful source of folate.

Some more ideas

- For a chocolate and chestnut meringue cake, melt 85 g (3 oz) good dark chocolate in a bowl set over a saucepan of hot water, then spread it over the flat side of one meringue. Leave to set. Mix 1 can sweetened chestnut purée, about 240 g, with 200 g (7 oz) fromage frais, and spread over the chocolate. Top with the other meringue, and decorate with chocolate curls.

- To make mini meringues, use ground hazelnuts or pistachios in the meringue mixture and shape it into ovals with 2 spoons, placing them on baking sheets lined with baking parchment. Bake for 50–60 minutes. Dip the base of each meringue in melted chocolate and sandwich pairs together with a mixture of 150 g (5½ oz) Greek-style yogurt or fromage frais and 150 ml (5 fl oz) whipped whipping cream.

Vanilla angel cake

Almost fat-free, this very light cake really is the food of angels. It is made using egg whites only, no yolks, and during baking develops a delicious golden crust that hides the tender, pure white interior. Here, it is served with creamy fromage frais and summer berries, but it is just as lovely with juicy peaches, mango or apricots.

Serves 10

115 g (4 oz) plain flour

85 g (3 oz) icing sugar

8 large egg whites, at room temperature

150 g (5½ oz) caster sugar

¼ tsp salt

1 tsp cream of tartar

1 tsp pure vanilla extract

To serve

225 g (8 oz) strawberries, cut into quarters

225 g (8 oz) raspberries

225 g (8 oz) blueberries

300 g (10½ oz) fromage frais

Preparation time: 15 minutes

Cooking time: 35 minutes

Each serving provides Ⓥ

kcal 190, **protein** 6 g, **fat** 2 g (of which saturated fat 1 g), **carbohydrate** 39 g (of which sugars 30 g), **fibre** 2 g

✓✓✓ C

✓　 B₂, B₁₂

1 Preheat the oven to 180°C (350°F, gas mark 4). Sift the flour and icing sugar onto a large plate and set aside.

2 Put the egg whites in a large bowl and whisk until quite frothy. Add the sugar, salt, cream of tartar and vanilla extract, and continue whisking until the mixture forms stiff peaks.

3 Sift the flour mixture over the egg whites and fold in very gently with a large metal spoon until well blended.

4 Spoon the mixture into an ungreased 25 cm (10 in) non-stick tube tin, making sure there are no air pockets. Bake for 35 minutes or until well risen, golden brown and springy to the touch.

5 Invert the cake, still in the tin, onto a wire rack and leave to cool completely, upside down. When it is cold, slide a long knife around the side of the tin to loosen the cake, then invert it onto a serving plate. (The cake can be kept, wrapped in cling film or stored in an airtight container, for 1–2 days.)

6 Just before serving, mix together the strawberries, raspberries and blueberries. Spoon the fruit into the hollow in the centre of the cake. Serve with the fromage frais in a bowl.

Some more ideas

● To make a lemon and lime angel cake, add the finely grated zest of 1 lemon and 1 lime to the beaten egg white with the sifted flour and icing sugar. While the cake is cooling, peel 2 small Cantaloupe melons and remove the seeds. Cut the melon into small chunks and place in a bowl. Squeeze the juice from the lemon and lime, sprinkle it over the melon and toss to coat well. Serve the cake with the melon pieces piled up in the centre.

● For a chocolate angel cake, sift 2 tbsp cocoa powder with the flour and icing sugar. Decorate the cake with a mixture of 1 tbsp cocoa powder and 1 tbsp icing sugar, sifted together.

● To make a coffee angel cake, sift 1 tbsp instant coffee powder (not granules) with the flour and icing sugar. Decorate with icing sugar.

Plus point

● Fromage frais is a useful source of calcium, which is an essential component of bones and teeth – the adult skeleton contains 1.2 kg (nearly 3 lb) calcium, and 99% of this is present in the bones. Calcium also plays an important role in the regulation of blood clotting, muscle contraction and nerve function.

Rich chocolate torte

A generous amount of good-quality dark chocolate makes this Continental-style cake beautifully moist and rich – just a small slice will satisfy any sweet tooth. It's perfect with a cup of coffee, or try it warm for dessert, with a spoonful of soured cream or Greek-style yogurt and some fresh berries.

Serves 10

170 g (6 oz) good dark chocolate (at least
   70% cocoa solids)
75 g (2½ oz) unsalted butter
4 eggs
100 g (3½ oz) light muscovado sugar
30 g (1 oz) plain flour

To decorate
cape gooseberries, papery skins folded back
   (optional)
icing sugar
cocoa powder

Preparation time: 20 minutes
Cooking time: 15–20 minutes

Each serving provides
kcal 230, **protein** 4 g, **fat** 14 g (of which
saturated fat 8 g), **carbohydrate** 24 g (of
which sugars 21 g), **fibre** 0 g

✓✓	B₁₂
✓	A, copper

1 Preheat the oven to 180°C (350°F, gas mark 4). Grease a 23 cm (9 in) springform cake tin and line it with greased greaseproof paper.

2 Break up the chocolate and put it in a heatproof bowl with the butter. Set the bowl over a pan of almost boiling water, making sure the water is not touching the base of the bowl. Leave to melt, then remove from the heat and stir the mixture until smooth.

3 Meanwhile, put the eggs and sugar in a large bowl and beat with an electric mixer until the mixture has increased considerably in volume and leaves a trail on the surface when the beaters are lifted out. (If using a hand whisk or rotary beater, set the bowl over a pan of almost boiling water, making sure the water is not touching the base of the bowl.)

4 Add the chocolate mixture to the whisked mixture and fold it in with a large metal spoon. Gradually sift the flour over the top of the egg and chocolate mixture, folding in until it is just combined.

5 Turn the mixture into the prepared cake tin, gently spreading it to the edges to level the surface. Bake for 15–20 minutes or until the top of the cake feels just firm to the touch. Leave to cool in the tin.

6 Remove the cake from the tin and peel away the lining paper. Cut into thin wedges for serving, decorating each with a cape gooseberry, if liked, and dusting the plates with sifted icing sugar and cocoa powder. The cake can be kept in the fridge for 2–3 days.

Some more ideas
● Use ground almonds instead of flour.
● If you're making the torte for a special dessert, drizzle 3 tbsp brandy or an orange liqueur such as Cointreau over the top after baking, then leave the cake to cool.

Plus points
● Scientists at the University of California have discovered that chocolate, particularly dark chocolate, contains significant amounts of phenols. These substances work as an antioxidant, helping to prevent the oxidation of harmful LDL cholesterol, which is the cholesterol responsible for clogging the arteries. A 1¼ oz piece of chocolate contains about the same amount of phenols as a glass of red wine.
● Cape gooseberries contain useful amounts of beta-carotene, vitamin C and potassium.

cakes for all occasions

56

Blueberry cheesecake

Compared to most cheesecakes, this version isn't particularly high in fat, as it uses cottage and curd cheeses instead of the traditional cream cheese, and is lightened by folding in whisked egg whites before baking. The delectable filling is set atop a crunchy digestive biscuit and oat base.

Serves 8

115 g (4 oz) digestive biscuits

2 tbsp jumbo oats

55 g (2 oz) unsalted butter, melted

200 g (7 oz) cottage cheese

200 g (7 oz) curd cheese

4 tbsp fromage frais

1 whole egg

2 eggs, separated

4 tsp cornflour

finely grated zest of 1 large lemon

115 g (4 oz) icing sugar, sifted

140 g (5 oz) blueberries

To decorate

55 g (2 oz) blueberries

fresh mint leaves

1 tbsp icing sugar, sifted

Preparation time: 25 minutes, plus cooling and chilling

Cooking time: 1½ hours

Each serving provides Ⓥ

kcal 325, **protein** 11 g, **fat** 17 g (of which saturated fat 9 g), **carbohydrate** 35 g (of which sugars 22 g), **fibre** 1 g

✓✓ A, B₁₂, C

✓ B₂, folate, zinc

1 Preheat the oven to 180°C (350°F, gas mark 4). Line the bottom of a 21 cm (8½ in) springform cake tin with baking parchment.

2 Make the biscuits into crumbs, either by crushing them in a food processor or by putting them in a strong plastic bag and crushing them with a rolling pin.

3 Mix together the crushed biscuits, oats and melted butter. Spread this mixture evenly over the bottom of the prepared tin, pressing down firmly, and set aside.

4 Put the cottage cheese in a food processor or blender and blend until smooth. Add the curd cheese, fromage frais, the whole egg, 2 egg yolks, cornflour and lemon zest. Blend briefly until evenly mixed. Tip the mixture into a bowl.

5 Whisk the 2 egg whites in a clean bowl until they form soft peaks. Gradually add the icing sugar, whisking until the meringue is thick and glossy. Gently fold half the meringue into the cheese mixture. Fold in the blueberries, followed by the rest of the meringue.

6 Pour the mixture over the biscuit base in the tin and bake for 30 minutes. Cover loosely with foil and reduce the oven temperature to 160°C (325°F, gas mark 3). Bake for a further

1 hour or until the cheesecake feels just set in the centre. Turn off the oven and leave the cheesecake inside to cool for 30 minutes, with the door slightly ajar – this helps to prevent cracking.

7 Transfer the cheesecake to a wire rack to cool completely, then chill until ready to serve. Run a knife around the side of the cheesecake to loosen it, then remove it from the tin. Peel off the lining paper and place the cheesecake on a serving plate. Decorate with the extra blueberries and a few fresh mint leaves, and finish with a light dusting of icing sugar.

Plus points

• Blueberries are a good source of vitamin C and, like cranberries, they contain compounds that have been shown to inhibit bacteria which can cause urinary-tract infections. Studies have suggested that these compounds may also help to protect against cataracts and glaucoma.

• Cottage cheese is high in protein but low in fat, and provides useful amounts of the B vitamins B₁, niacin, B₆ and B₁₂.

Some more ideas

● Use ginger nuts or oatmeal cookies instead of digestive biscuits.

● Make a sponge instead of the biscuit base. Follow steps 2 and 3 of Summer fruit Swiss roll on page 30, but using 1 egg, 30 g (1 oz) caster sugar and 30 g (1 oz) plain flour. Bake the mixture in the springform tin in a preheated 200°C (400°F, gas mark 6) oven for 10 minutes or until well risen and pale golden.

● For a red fruit cheesecake, make the filling as in the main recipe, but omitting the blueberries. For the topping, gently heat 55 g (2 oz) sugar with 120 ml (4 fl oz) water in a saucepan until dissolved. Add 170 g (6 oz) stoned cherries and simmer for 3 minutes or until just softened.

Remove the cherries with a draining spoon. Mix 1 tbsp arrowroot with 1 tbsp cherry or orange liqueur or water. Add to the pan and simmer for 2 minutes or until the liquid is clear and thickened. Leave to cool for 5 minutes, then stir in the cherries, 115 g (4 oz) raspberries and 115 g (4 oz) halved small strawberries. Leave to cool before spooning over the cheesecake.

Small Cakes, Muffins and Scones

A tempting range of sweet and savoury morsels

IF YOU ARE NEW TO BAKING or if you are cooking with children, small cakes are an ideal choice. Quick and easy to prepare, they will fill your kitchen with delicious aromas, and cool down quickly so that eager helpers can enjoy the fruits of their labour. Fairy cakes with a light ricotta topping will be popular at children's parties. Sweet muffins, packed with good things such as fresh and dried fruit and yogurt, make a satisfying start to the day, while nothing can beat a scone with a cup of tea. Savoury muffins and scones are great with soup or salad for lunch.

Apple and muesli rock cakes

A little diced apple makes these rock cakes moist and fruity. Quick and easy to prepare, they are ideal to cook with younger members of the family, who will enjoy making them as much as eating them. Cooking is not only fun for children but also encourages them to be more aware of the foods they eat.

Makes 24 cakes

225 g (8 oz) self-raising flour

100 g (3½ oz) unsalted butter, cut into small pieces

55 g (2 oz) light muscovado sugar, plus a little extra to sprinkle

1 tsp ground cinnamon

2 dessert apples, peeled and diced

75 g (2½ oz) sugar-free muesli

1 egg, beaten

4–5 tbsp semi-skimmed milk, as needed

Preparation time: 20 minutes
Cooking time: 15 minutes

1 Preheat the oven to 190°C (375°F, gas mark 5). Put the flour into a bowl, add the butter and rub it in with your fingertips until the mixture resembles fine breadcrumbs.

2 Stir in the sugar, cinnamon, diced apples and muesli. Add the egg and stir it in with enough milk to bind the mixture together roughly.

3 Drop dessertspoonfuls of the mixture onto 2 greased baking sheets, leaving space around each cake, and sprinkle with a little extra sugar. Bake for 15 minutes or until golden and firm to the touch.

4 Transfer to a wire rack to cool, and serve warm or cold. The rock cakes can be kept in an airtight tin for up to 2 days.

Some more ideas

● Replace the muesli with a mixture of 3 tbsp rolled oats, 2 tbsp sesame or sunflower seeds and 55 g (2 oz) roughly chopped hazelnuts or almonds.

● For apple and mincemeat rock cakes, use just 1 peeled and diced dessert apple with 150 g (5½ oz) mincemeat, and substitute 75 g (2½ oz) rolled oats for the muesli. Omit the cinnamon.

● For tropical rock cakes, replace the apples, muesli and cinnamon with 50 g (1¾ oz) desiccated coconut and 170 g (6 oz) chopped ready-to-eat exotic dried fruits, including pineapple, papaya and mango.

Plus points

● Apples are a good source of vitamin C and soluble fibre (in the form of pectin), as well as offering a flavonoid called quercetin, which is thought to have a potent antioxidant effect.

● Adding muesli to cakes and bakes is a good way to increase their fibre content.

● Children need healthy snacks to boost their energy and nutritional needs, and these little rock cakes are much better than sugar-laden commercial biscuits or salty crisps.

Each cake provides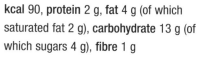
kcal 90, **protein** 2 g, **fat** 4 g (of which saturated fat 2 g), **carbohydrate** 13 g (of which sugars 4 g), **fibre** 1 g

small cakes, muffins and scones

Iced fairy cakes

Fairy cakes are easy to prepare and always popular with children. Using ricotta in the topping makes a lighter, fresher alternative to the more usual glacé icing. The cakes are best iced shortly before serving.

Makes 18 cakes

125 g (4½ oz) unsalted butter, at room
    temperature
125 g (4½ oz) caster sugar
2 eggs
100 g (3½ oz) self-raising white flour
30 g (1 oz) self-raising wholemeal flour
½ tsp baking powder
finely grated zest of ½ orange
30 g (1 oz) ready-to-eat dried apricots,
    thinly sliced, to decorate

Orange ricotta icing

250 g (8½ oz) ricotta cheese
55 g (2 oz) icing sugar
finely grated zest of ½ orange

Preparation time: 20 minutes
Cooking time: 20 minutes

1 Preheat the oven to 180°C (350°F, gas mark 4). Line a 12-cup and a 6-cup patty tin or shallow bun tin with paper cake cases.

2 Put the butter, sugar and eggs in a large bowl. Sift the white and wholemeal flours and the baking powder into the bowl, tipping in any bran left in the sieve. Add the orange zest and beat with a hand-held electric mixer for 2 minutes or until smooth and creamy.

3 Divide the mixture among the paper cake cases. Bake for about 20 minutes or until just firm to the touch. Transfer to a wire rack to cool. (The un-iced cakes can be stored in an airtight container for up to 2 days.)

4 To make the icing, put the ricotta in a bowl and sift in the icing sugar. Add the orange zest and beat with a wooden spoon until well mixed.

5 Spread a little icing over the top of each cake and decorate with a couple of dried apricot slices. Serve as soon as possible after icing.

Some more ideas

● Add 75 g (2½ oz) chopped ready-to-eat dried apricots to the mixture at the end of step 2.

● For chocolate-iced fairy cakes, melt 75 g (2½ oz) good-quality milk chocolate in a heatproof bowl set over a pan of almost simmering water, then spread it over the cooled cakes instead of the ricotta icing.

● To make queen cakes, substitute the finely grated zest of 1 lemon for the orange zest and stir in 75 g (2½ oz) raisins at the end of step 2. Omit the icing and instead lightly dust the cakes with sifted icing sugar once they have cooled.

Plus points

● Using a mixture of wholemeal flour and white flour increases the fibre content of the cakes without making them too heavy.

● Dried apricots are one of the richest fruit sources of iron, and they provide soluble fibre.

● The ricotta icing uses much less sugar than traditional glacé icing.

Each cake provides Ⓥ

kcal 150, **protein** 3 g, **fat** 8 g (of which saturated fat 5 g), **carbohydrate** 17 g (of which sugars 11 g), **fibre** 0.5 g

✓   A, B$_{12}$

Breakfast muffins

American-style muffins are perfect for breakfast, providing the energy boost the body needs to start the day. This particular recipe is packed full of good ingredients that add fibre, vitamins and minerals too.

Makes 12 muffins

85 g (3 oz) plain wholemeal flour
150 g (5½ oz) plain white flour
2 tsp bicarbonate of soda
pinch of salt
¼ tsp ground cinnamon
55 g (2 oz) dark molasses sugar
30 g (1 oz) wheatgerm
170 g (6 oz) raisins
225 g (8 oz) plain low-fat yogurt
4 tbsp sunflower oil
1 egg
grated zest of ½ orange
3 tbsp orange juice

Preparation time: 15 minutes
Cooking time: 15–20 minutes

1 Preheat the oven to 200°C (400°F, gas mark 6). Grease a 12-cup deep muffin tray – each cup should measure 6–7.5 cm (2½–3 in) across the top and be 2.5–4 cm (1–1½ in) deep.

2 Sift the wholemeal and white flours, bicarbonate of soda, salt and cinnamon into a bowl, tipping in any bran left in the sieve. Stir in the sugar, wheatgerm and raisins, and make a well in the centre.

3 Lightly whisk together the yogurt, oil, egg, and orange zest and juice. Pour into the well in the dry ingredients and stir together, mixing only enough to moisten the dry ingredients. Do not beat or overmix.

4 Spoon the mixture into the muffin tray, dividing it equally among the cups. Bake for 15–20 minutes or until the muffins are well risen and just firm to the touch. Leave them to cool in the tray for 2–3 minutes, then turn out onto a wire rack. The muffins are best eaten freshly baked, preferably still slightly warm from the oven, but can be cooled completely and then kept in an airtight tin for up to 2 days.

Some more ideas

● Substitute chopped prunes or dried dates for the raisins.

● For carrot and spice muffins, replace the cinnamon with 1½ tsp mixed spice. Stir 100 g (3½ oz) grated carrot into the flour mixture with the wheatgerm, and reduce the amount of raisins to 115 g (4 oz).

● To make blueberry and walnut muffins, instead of raisins use 200 g (7 oz) blueberries, and add 100 g (3½ oz) chopped walnuts.

Plus points

● Breakfast is a good opportunity to top up the fibre intake for the day, which is why eating a high-fibre cereal is usually recommended. These muffins are another good choice, as they offer plenty of dietary fibre from the wholemeal flour, wheatgerm and raisins.

● Wheatgerm is the embryo of the wheat grain and as such contains a high concentration of nutrients, intended to nourish the growing plant. Just 1 tbsp of wheatgerm provides around 25% of the average daily requirement for vitamin B_6. Wheatgerm is also a good source of folate, vitamin E, zinc and magnesium.

Each muffin provides

kcal 180, **protein** 4 g, **fat** 5 g (of which saturated fat 1 g), **carbohydrate** 31 g (of which sugars 17 g), **fibre** 2 g

✓ B_1, B_6, E, calcium, iron, selenium, zinc

Banana cinnamon muffins

These delicious, moist muffins with a crunchy sweet topping, are not only low in fat but also contain bananas, oat bran, soya milk and soya flour – all beneficial ingredients for anyone eating for a healthy heart. Enjoy the muffins warm for breakfast or at coffee or tea time.

Makes 12 muffins

55 g (2 oz) oat bran
2 tsp ground cinnamon
1 tbsp demerara sugar
200 ml (7 fl oz) soya milk
3 bananas
125 g (4½ oz) light muscovado sugar
3 tbsp sunflower oil
2 tsp pure vanilla extract
1 egg white
200 g (7 oz) plain flour
55 g (2 oz) soya flour
1 tbsp baking powder

Preparation time: 15 minutes
Cooking time: 20–25 minutes

1 Preheat the oven to 180ºC (350ºF, gas mark 4). Line a 12-cup deep muffin tray with paper muffin cases.

2 Mix together 2 tsp of the oat bran, 1 tsp of the cinnamon and all of the demerara sugar, and set aside for the topping. Place the remaining oat bran in a bowl with the soya milk and leave to soak for 5 minutes.

3 Peel and roughly mash the bananas. Add the brown sugar, oil, vanilla extract and egg white, and beat well together.

4 Sift the plain and soya flours, baking powder and remaining cinnamon into a bowl. Make a well in the centre and stir in the soaked oat bran and the banana mixture. Mix lightly but thoroughly, just until smooth.

5 Spoon the mixture into the paper cases and sprinkle with the topping. Bake for 20–25 minutes or until well risen and golden brown. Lift the muffins out of the tray onto a wire rack to cool a bit. Serve fresh, preferably still slightly warm from the oven. These muffins are best eaten on the day they are made.

Some more ideas

● Children love mini-muffins, which make healthy snacks. Use 18 small paper cake cases and reduce the baking time to 15–20 minutes.
● For raspberry ginger muffins, replace the cinnamon with ground ginger, and stir 2 tbsp chopped candied ginger and 115 g (4 oz) fresh raspberries into the batter at the end of step 4.

Plus points

● Diets rich in soya protein are believed to help reduce high blood cholesterol levels. Several studies suggest that soya products may also help to reduce the risk of heart disease, certain cancers and osteoporosis, as well as alleviating symptoms associated with the menopause.
● Bananas contain a type of dietary fibre called fructoligosaccarides (FOS), which is believed to stimulate the growth of friendly bacteria in the gut while inhibiting the growth of harmful bacteria.
● Oat bran is an excellent source of soluble fibre, which helps to counteract the build-up of cholesterol in the blood and control blood sugar levels.

Each muffin provides

kcal 185, **protein** 5 g, **fat** 5 g (of which saturated fat 0.5 g), **carbohydrate** 33 g (of which sugars 18 g), **fibre** 3 g

✓　B₁, B₆, folate, copper, zinc

small cakes, muffins and scones

Mediterranean herb muffins

Here's a savoury version of American-style muffins, speckled with fresh herbs and spring onions and flavoured with Parmesan cheese. With their sponge-like texture, they make an interesting alternative to bread, to serve with grilled vegetables, soups and salads. Eat them plain or spread with a soft cheese such as quark or ricotta.

Makes 12 muffins

225 g (8 oz) plain flour
1 tbsp baking powder
¼ tsp salt
1 tbsp chopped fresh thyme
small handful of fresh basil leaves, torn into
    small pieces
75 g (2½ oz) fine cornmeal or instant polenta,
    plus a little extra to sprinkle
3 spring onions, thinly sliced
55 g (2 oz) Parmesan cheese, finely grated
4 tbsp extra virgin olive oil
140 g (5 oz) plain low-fat yogurt
170 ml (6 fl oz) semi-skimmed milk
2 eggs

Preparation time: 15 minutes
Cooking time: 20 minutes

1 Preheat the oven to 190ºC (375ºF, gas mark 5). Line a 12-cup deep muffin tray with paper muffin cases.

2 Sift the flour, baking powder and salt into a large bowl. Stir in the thyme, basil, cornmeal or polenta, spring onions and Parmesan until evenly combined.

3 In another bowl, beat together the olive oil, yogurt, milk and eggs. Pour the egg mixture over the dry ingredients and stir gently until the dry ingredients are just moistened. There should still be a little dry flour visible.

4 Spoon the mixture into the paper cases. Sprinkle with a little extra cornmeal or polenta, then bake for about 20 minutes or until the muffins are well risen, pale golden and just firm to the touch. Transfer to a wire rack to cool. Serve fresh, preferably still slightly warm from the oven. These muffins are best eaten within 24 hours; store in an airtight tin.

Some more ideas

• To make 18 smaller snack-size muffins, use ordinary paper cake cases and bake them for 15–18 minutes.
• Replace the fresh thyme and basil with 1½ tsp dried herbes de Provence.
• For Parmesan and leek muffins, replace the spring onions and herbs with 1 finely chopped small leek (about 150 g/5½ oz). Cook it in 15 g (½ oz) butter for 3 minutes or until softened but not coloured, then allow to cool before adding to the mixture.

Plus points

• Parmesan is a high-fat cheese, but it offers plenty of flavour so can be used in modest quantities and still have a big impact.
• As well as being a basic flavouring ingredient in almost all savoury dishes, onions have many health benefits. Recent research suggests that they contain a sulphur compound which can help to lower blood cholesterol levels and lessen the risk of blood clots forming, so reducing the risk of coronary heart disease.
• Many herbs have medicinal properties in addition to their culinary uses. Herbalists prescribe basil to help soothe cramps, upset stomachs and flatulence.

Each muffin provides

kcal 170, **protein** 6 g, **fat** 7 g (of which saturated fat 2 g), **carbohydrate** 21 g (of which sugars 2 g), **fibre** 1 g

✓✓	B₁₂
✓	calcium, zinc

Blackberry and lemon scones

Make these scones in the autumn when firm, sweet blackberries are in season. The addition of buttermilk to the mixture ensures the result is light and flaky. Serve fresh from the oven for a deliciously different tea-time scone.

Makes 8 scone wedges

115 g (4 oz) self-raising white flour, plus extra to sprinkle

115 g (4 oz) self-raising wholemeal flour

1 tsp baking powder

55 g (2 oz) caster sugar

55 g (2 oz) unsalted butter, cut into small pieces

finely grated zest of 1 lemon

85 g (3 oz) small, firm, fresh blackberries

120 ml (4 fl oz) buttermilk, or more as needed

Preparation time: 15 minutes
Cooking time: 20–25 minutes

1 Preheat the oven to 200°C (400°F, gas mark 6). Sift the white and wholemeal flours and the baking powder into a large bowl, tipping in any bran left in the sieve. Stir in the sugar. Add the butter and rub it in with your fingertips until the mixture resembles fine breadcrumbs.

2 Stir in the lemon zest, then very gently stir in the blackberries. Do not overmix, as the blackberries can easily become crushed.

3 Lightly stir in the buttermilk using a round-bladed knife, again being careful not to crush the blackberries. If there are any dry bits of dough in the bottom of the bowl, add a little more buttermilk. As soon as the mixture comes together in a soft dough, lift it from the bowl onto a floured surface and knead gently 2 or 3 times only, just to form a rough ball.

4 Pat out the dough carefully with your hands to make an 18 cm (7 in) round. Transfer it to a greased baking sheet. Mark into 8 wedges with the back of a knife and sprinkle with a little extra white flour. Bake for 20–25 minutes or until pale golden and risen. Serve warm, broken into the marked wedges. These scones are best eaten freshly baked, or on the day they are made, but will still be good the next day; store them in an airtight tin.

Some more ideas

● For blueberry scones, substitute fresh blueberries for the blackberries.

● To make cinnamon raisin scones, substitute 55 g (2 oz) raisins for the blackberries and ½ tsp ground cinnamon for the lemon zest. Increase the quantity of buttermilk to 150 ml (5 fl oz). Roll out the dough to a thickness of 2.5 cm (1 in) and stamp out rounds using a 5–6 cm (2–2½ in) plain cutter. Put them on a greased baking sheet and brush with 1 tbsp semi-skimmed milk mixed with 2 tsp caster sugar to glaze. Bake for 12–15 minutes or until risen and golden.

Plus points

● Blackberries are high in fibre and vitamin C, and are one of the richest fruit sources of vitamin E.

● Traditionally buttermilk is the liquid left over after cream has been turned into butter by churning. However, these days it is usually made by adding a bacterial culture to skimmed milk. Buttermilk is extremely low in fat (0.2–0.5 g fat per 100 ml/3½ fl oz).

Each scone provides Ⓥ

kcal 180, **protein** 4 g, **fat** 6 g (of which saturated fat 4 g), **carbohydrate** 29 g (of which sugars 9 g), **fibre** 2 g

✓ B₁, B₆, selenium

Drop scones

Drop scones, also called Scotch pancakes, are easy and fun to make, and perfect for tea or even as a simple dessert. Served with creamy fromage frais and sweet, succulent berries, they are quite irresistible.

Makes about 24 drop scones

125 g (4½ oz) self-raising flour

2 tsp caster sugar

1 egg, beaten

1 tbsp melted unsalted butter

150 ml (5 fl oz) semi-skimmed milk

4 tsp sunflower oil

To serve

100 g (3½ oz) blueberries

1 tsp clear honey

100 g (3½ oz) raspberries

200 g (7 oz) fromage frais

Preparation time: 10 minutes

Cooking time: 15–20 minutes

Each scone provides

kcal 55, **protein** 2 g, **fat** 2 g (of which saturated fat 1 g), **carbohydrate** 6 g (of which sugars 2 g), **fibre** 0.5 g

✓ B$_{12}$

1 Put the flour in a bowl and stir in the sugar. Make a well in the centre, and add the egg, melted butter and a little of the milk. Gradually stir the flour into the liquids and add the remaining milk a little at a time, to make a fairly thick, smooth batter.

2 Heat a large shallow dish in a low oven, then turn off the heat and line the dish with a tea-towel (this is for keeping the cooked drop scones warm). Heat a griddle or large, heavy-based frying pan over a moderate heat and grease it with 1 tsp of the oil.

3 Using a dessertspoon, pour the batter from the pointed end (rather than the side of the spoon) to make neat, round drop scones. Depending on the size of the griddle, you should be able to cook 4–6 scones at once, but make sure you leave enough space round them so you can turn them easily. Cook for about 2 minutes or until almost set and bubbles are breaking on the surface; the scones should be golden brown underneath.

4 Using a palette knife, turn the scones over and cook for a further 1–2 minutes or until golden brown on the other side. Transfer to the prepared dish, wrap in the tea-towel and keep warm while you cook the remaining scones. Grease the griddle lightly with 1 tsp oil before cooking each batch.

5 Place the blueberries in a bowl and stir in the honey. Add the raspberries and lightly crush the fruit, leaving some berries whole. Serve the scones warm with the honeyed berries and the fromage frais.

Some more ideas

● Instead of serving the drop scones with fromage frais and crushed fruit, top each one with a dab of Greek-style yogurt and a little jam.

● To make apple drop scones, stir 1 cored and finely diced dessert apple into the batter with a pinch of ground cloves. Serve the scones dusted with a little sifted icing sugar.

● To make savoury Parmesan and herb drop scones, instead of caster sugar add 1 tbsp snipped fresh chives, 1 tbsp chopped fresh oregano and 2 tbsp freshly grated Parmesan cheese to the flour. Serve the drop scones topped with a little soft cheese and halved cherry tomatoes.

Plus points

● Home-made drop scones contain less fat and sugar than bought scones, and serving them with fromage frais instead of butter keeps the total fat content low.

● Milk is a good source of calcium, essential for healthy bones and teeth. It also supplies protein, and vitamins B$_2$ and B$_{12}$

small cakes, muffins and scones

Potato scones

Served fresh from the oven while still slightly warm, scones are a traditional favourite, whether for tea-time, lunch or a quick snack. Here, mashed potato is added to the mixture, which makes these savoury scones wonderfully moist and improves their keeping qualities. It's a great way of using up leftover potato.

Makes 6 scone wedges

225 g (8 oz) self-raising flour

½ tsp salt

¼ tsp mustard powder

1½ tsp baking powder

30 g (1 oz) butter, cut into small pieces

4 tbsp semi-skimmed milk, or more as needed

170 g (6 oz) cold mashed potato (without any milk or butter added)

To finish

milk or beaten egg to glaze

2 tsp medium oatmeal

Preparation time: 10 minutes

Cooking time: 15–20 minutes

Each scone provides

kcal 210, **protein** 5 g, **fat** 5 g (of which saturated fat 3 g), **carbohydrate** 36 g (of which sugars 1 g), **fibre** 1.5 g

✓ A, B₁, B₆, calcium

1 Preheat the oven to 220°C (425°F, gas mark 7). Sift the flour, salt, mustard powder and baking powder into a bowl. Rub in the butter with your fingertips until the mixture resembles fine breadcrumbs.

2 In another bowl, stir the milk into the mashed potato, mixing well. Add to the dry ingredients and stir with a fork to mix, adding another 1–2 tbsp milk, if needed, to make a soft dough.

3 Lightly knead the dough on a floured surface for a few seconds or until smooth, then roll out to a 15 cm (6 in) round about 2 cm (¾ in) thick. Place on a greased baking sheet. Mark the scone round into 6 wedges with a sharp knife.

4 Brush with milk or beaten egg, then sprinkle with the oatmeal. Bake for 15–20 minutes or until well risen and golden brown.

5 Transfer to a wire rack and break into wedges. Serve warm or leave to cool. The scones can be kept in an airtight tin for up to 3 days. If liked, reheat them for serving: set on a baking sheet, cover with foil and warm in a low oven for about 5 minutes.

Some more ideas

• Instead of oatmeal, dust the scones with a mixture of 2 tsp plain flour and a pinch of paprika before baking.

• For potato and feta scones, instead of butter stir 75 g (2½ oz) feta cheese, finely crumbled, and 2 tbsp snipped fresh chives into the dry ingredients.

• Make spiced sweet potato scones, using mashed sweet potato instead of ordinary potato. Replace the mustard powder with freshly grated nutmeg or ground cardamom. These scones will be sweeter than those in the main recipe.

Plus point

• Potatoes are surprisingly high in vitamin C, and eaten regularly they can make a significant contribution of this essential nutrient to the diet. In addition to its antioxidant properties that play an important role in the prevention of cancer and heart disease, vitamin C may help to reduce the severity of the common cold. Potatoes are also an excellent source of starchy carbohydrate, provide fibre and potassium, and are low in fat.

Cheese and watercress scones

Peppery watercress and mature Cheddar flavour these tempting and nutritious savoury scones. Serve them warm with soup instead of bread or split and fill them with salad ingredients for a satisfying packed lunch.

Makes 8 scones

140 g (5 oz) self-raising white flour

140 g (5 oz) self-raising wholemeal flour

1 tsp baking powder

50 g (1¾ oz) butter, cut into small pieces

50 g (1¾ oz) rolled oats

85 g (3 oz) watercress without coarse stalks, chopped

75 g (2½ oz) mature Cheddar cheese, grated

100 ml (3½ fl oz) semi-skimmed milk, plus a little extra to glaze

salt and pepper

Preparation time: 20 minutes

Cooking time: 10–15 minutes

1 Preheat the oven to 230°C (450°F, gas mark 8). Sift the white and wholemeal flours and the baking powder into a bowl, then tip in any bran left in the sieve. Rub in the butter with your fingertips until the mixture resembles fine breadcrumbs.

2 Add the rolled oats, watercress, about three-quarters of the cheese, and a little salt and pepper. Use a fork to stir in the milk. Scrape the dough together with a spatula and turn out onto a well-floured surface. Pat together into a smooth, soft ball. It will be a little softer than a standard scone dough.

3 Pat or roll out the dough to 2 cm (¾ in) thick. With a 7.5 cm (3 in) round cutter, stamp out the scones. Press the trimmings together lightly, re-roll and stamp out more scones.

4 Place the scones on a greased baking sheet, arranging them so they are not touching. Brush the tops lightly with milk and sprinkle with the remaining grated cheese. Bake for 10–15 minutes or until risen and golden brown. Cool on a wire rack. These scones are at their best eaten on the day they are made, but will still be good the next day; store in an airtight tin.

Some more ideas

● To make a scone round, place the smooth ball of dough on a greased baking tray and press it out into a flat round 2–2.5 cm (¾–1 in) thick. Use a sharp knife to cut the dough into 8 wedges, leaving them in place. Bake for about 15 minutes or until risen and golden.

● For cheese and celery scones, replace the watercress with 2 celery sticks, finely chopped.

● To make carrot and poppy seed scones, instead of watercress and cheese, add 50 g (1¾ oz) finely grated carrot and 1 tbsp poppy seeds with the oats. Before baking, sprinkle the top of the scones with 1 tbsp poppy seeds instead of cheese.

Plus points

● These scones are a good source of fibre – both the insoluble type found in wholemeal flour and soluble fibre from the oats.

● Cheddar cheese is a good source of protein and a valuable source of calcium, phosphorus and the B vitamins B_{12} and niacin.

● Watercress provides beta-carotene, vitamin C and vitamin E, nutrients that act as protective antioxidants. It also contains a compound that has been shown to have antibiotic properties.

Each scone provides Ⓥ

kcal 230, **protein** 8 g, **fat** 10 g (of which saturated fat 5 g), **carbohydrate** 30 g (of which sugars 1 g), **fibre** 3 g

✓✓　A

✓　B_1, B_6, B_{12}, C, folate, calcium, copper, iron, selenium, zinc

Ricotta herb scones

These craggy-topped, savoury rolls are made with self-raising flour, soft cheese and plenty of fresh herbs –
ideally a mixture of flat-leaf parsley, chives, thyme and rosemary, although any favourite combination will do.
The scones are nicest eaten warm from the oven, with soup or salad.

Makes 8 scones

450 g (1 lb) self-raising flour
½ tsp salt
several grinds of black pepper
225 g (8 oz) ricotta cheese
1 egg
3 tbsp chopped mixed fresh herbs
240 ml (8 fl oz) semi-skimmed milk, or as
   needed, plus extra to glaze
1 tbsp sesame seeds

Preparation time: 20 minutes
Cooking time: 20–25 minutes

1 Preheat the oven to 190°C (375°F, gas mark 5). Sift the flour into a mixing bowl and stir in the salt and black pepper.

2 Put the ricotta, egg and herbs into another bowl and stir well until smooth. Add to the flour and stir in with a round-bladed knife. Work in enough of the milk to make a slightly soft but not sticky dough.

3 Turn the dough out onto a lightly floured work surface and knead gently for 1 minute or until smooth. Divide into 8 equal portions and shape each into a rough-looking ball.

4 Place the scones on a large greased baking sheet, arranging them so they are not touching. Brush lightly with milk to glaze and sprinkle with the sesame seeds. Bake for 20–25 minutes or until the scones are lightly browned and sound hollow when they are tapped on the base.

5 Transfer to a wire rack and leave to cool for a few minutes. Or, if not eating warm, allow to cool completely. The scones can be kept in an airtight tin for up to 24 hours.

Some more ideas

● Use plain cottage cheese instead of ricotta.
● Rather than a mixture of herbs, use just one kind, such as flat-leaf parsley or chives. Another good choice is finely shredded fresh basil.
● To make goat's cheese, olive and thyme scones, replace the ricotta with soft fresh goat's cheese, and the mixed fresh herbs with 2 tbsp chopped black olives and 1 tbsp chopped fresh thyme.

Each scone provides

kcal 280, **protein** 11 g, **fat** 7 g (of which saturated fat 3 g), **carbohydrate** 46 g (of which sugars 3 g), **fibre** 2 g

✓✓✓	B₁₂
✓✓	B₁, calcium
✓	A, B₂, B₆, folate, copper, iron, zinc

Plus points

● Ricotta, which is made from the whey drained off when making cheeses such as mozzarella, has a high moisture content. This makes it lower in fat and calories than most other soft, creamy cheeses.
● Using fresh herbs in cooking helps to reduce the need for salt. Salt is an acquired taste. If you gradually reduce the amount you use, your palate will adapt, as the salt receptors on the tongue become much more sensitive to it. This process takes about 4 weeks, but you'll eventually find you prefer foods with less salt.

Biscuits and Bars

Scrumptious snacks and nibbles

IT'S HARD TO RESIST A BISCUIT, particularly if it's home-made. Not only will it taste better than most commercial biscuits, but it will be much better for you, too. There are plenty of ideas here for filling the biscuit tin with sweet treats that won't sabotage a healthy diet. Children's favourites such as chocolate chip cookies, flapjacks and brownies are updated to make a wholesome alternative to bought sugary snacks. And there are biscuits that adults will find hard to resist, such as cranberry and almond biscotti scented with cinnamon, and wonderfully fruity fig rolls. There's also a really easy recipe for digestives that will knock spots off the ones you buy in the shops.

Digestive biscuits

These crunchy, golden biscuits are full of nutty, slightly sweet flavours. They are sliced from a long piece of dough, which you can make ahead and store in the fridge or freezer. Bake the biscuits all at once or in batches, keeping the remainder of the dough chilled. It will keep for 2 months in the freezer.

Makes 25 biscuits

150 g (5½ oz) plain wholemeal flour

1 tsp baking powder

½ tsp salt

½ tsp bicarbonate of soda

30 g (1 oz) medium oatmeal

20 g (¾ oz) bran

100 g (3½ oz) dark muscovado sugar

50 g (1¾ oz) unsalted butter, cut into small pieces

4 tbsp milk, or as needed

Preparation time: 15 minutes, plus 30 minutes chilling

Cooking time: 12 minutes

Each biscuit provides Ⓥ

kcal 60, **protein** 1 g, **fat** 2 g (of which saturated fat 1 g), **carbohydrate** 9 g (of which sugars 4 g), **fibre** 1 g

1 Sift the flour, baking powder, salt and bicarbonate of soda into a mixing bowl, tipping in any bran left in the sieve. Add the oatmeal, bran and sugar, and mix well to combine.

2 Add the butter and rub it in with your fingertips until the mixture resembles breadcrumbs. Add 3 tbsp of the milk and stir it in well so the mixture comes together to form a soft dough. If the mixture is a little dry, add the remaining 1 tbsp milk.

3 Turn the dough out onto a sheet of greaseproof paper and shape it into a log about 25 cm (10 in) long. Wrap the paper round the dough and roll it gently back and forth to make a smooth shape. Twist the ends of the paper together to seal. Chill the dough for about 30 minutes. (It can be kept for up to 4 days in the fridge.)

4 Preheat the oven to 190°C (375°F, gas mark 5). Unwrap the dough and, using a very sharp knife, cut it across into slices 8 mm (⅓ in) thick. Use the greaseproof paper to line a baking sheet, and place the biscuits on it. Bake for about 12 minutes or until lightly browned.

5 Transfer the biscuits to a wire rack and leave to cool completely. They can be kept in an airtight tin for up to 5 days.

Some more ideas

● To make lemon sesame biscuits, toast 1 tbsp sesame seeds in a dry frying pan over a moderate heat for about 5 minutes or until golden, stirring constantly. Turn them out onto a plate and cool. Stir them into the mixture, together with the finely grated zest of 1 lemon, before adding the milk.

● For spiced digestive biscuits, stir in ½ tsp finely ground black pepper, ¼ tsp ground cinnamon, ¼ tsp freshly grated nutmeg and ¼ tsp ground allspice before adding the milk.

Plus points

● With only 50 g (1¾ oz) butter, these biscuits are remarkably low in saturated fat.

● Using a blend of wholemeal flour, oatmeal and bran provides a great dose of healthy dietary fibre in the most delicious way.

● Muscovado is an unrefined sugar produced from raw sugar cane. Dark muscovado retains more molasses, a by-product of the sugar-making process, than light muscovado and other lighter unrefined sugars, and thus more of the nutrients in molasses – vitamin B_6, magnesium, iron and calcium.

Oatmeal and raisin cookies

Both children and adults will love these crisp, melt-in-the-mouth cookies. They are a really wholesome treat, lower in fat and sugar than most bought cookies, and packed with oatmeal and raisins for extra nutrients and flavour. It's worth making a double batch and freezing some – they'll keep for 2 months and thaw in minutes.

Makes 18 cookies

85 g (3 oz) unsalted butter, at room
    temperature
115 g (4 oz) light muscovado sugar
1 egg, beaten
115 g (4 oz) self-raising flour
55 g (2 oz) medium oatmeal
170 g (6 oz) raisins

Preparation time: 15 minutes
Cooking time: 10–15 minutes

1 Preheat the oven to 180°C (350°F, gas mark 4). Beat the butter and sugar together until pale and fluffy, then gradually beat in the egg. Sift in the flour, then fold it in with the oatmeal and raisins.

2 Drop heaped teaspoonfuls of the mixture onto 3 greased baking sheets, leaving enough space around each cookie to allow it to spread during baking.

3 Bake for 10–15 minutes or until golden brown. Cool slightly on the baking sheets, then transfer to a wire rack and leave to cool completely. These cookies can be kept in an airtight container for 3–4 days.

Some more ideas

• Add the finely grated zest of 1 small lemon or orange to the mixture with the oatmeal and raisins.

• Sift in 1–1½ tsp ground mixed spice, cinnamon or ginger with the flour.

• For low-sugar oatmeal cookies, add a banana for sweetening and use just 55 g (2 oz) sugar. After beating the sugar with the butter, beat in 1 mashed banana (about 85 g/3 oz).

Plus points

• Raisins are a useful source of iron, potassium and fibre as well as natural sugar. If you serve these cookies with a glass of freshly squeezed orange or pink grapefruit juice, the vitamin C in the fruit juice will help the body absorb the iron in the raisins.

• Oatmeal is an excellent source of soluble fibre, which can help to reduce high blood cholesterol levels, thereby reducing the risk of heart disease. Soluble fibre also helps to slow the absorption of carbohydrate into the bloodstream, resulting in a gentler rise and fall in blood sugar levels.

Each cookie provides
kcal 125, **protein** 1.5 g, **fat** 4.5 g (of which saturated fat 3 g), **carbohydrate** 20 g (of which sugars 13 g), **fibre** 1 g

biscuits and bars

Ginger nuts

Here's a healthier version of a traditional favourite. Bake quick round biscuits, or buy some fancy cutters and encourage children to have a go at making gingerbread figures, stars or Christmas trees, and give them dried fruit or nut decorations. Whatever the shape, theses spicy, crunchy biscuits taste terrific.

Makes 12 biscuits

85 g (3 oz) plain white flour
85 g (3 oz) plain wholemeal flour
½ tsp bicarbonate of soda
2 tsp ground ginger
½ tsp ground cinnamon
50 g (1¾ oz) butter
4 tbsp golden syrup

Preparation time: 15 minutes
Cooking time: 8–10 minutes

1 Preheat the oven to 190°C (375°F, gas mark 5). Sift the white and wholemeal flours, bicarbonate of soda, ginger and cinnamon into a bowl, tipping in any bran left in the sieve.

2 Put the butter and golden syrup in a small pan and melt over a low heat, stirring occasionally. Pour the melted mixture onto the dry ingredients and stir to bind them together into a firm dough.

3 Break off a walnut-sized lump of dough and roll it into a ball on the palm of your hand. Press it flat into a thick biscuit, about 6 cm (2½ in) in diameter, and place on a greased baking sheet. Repeat with the remaining dough. (Or roll out the dough and stamp out decorative shapes; see Some more ideas, right.)

4 Bake the biscuits for 8–10 minutes or until they are slightly risen and browned. Leave to cool on the baking sheet for 2–3 minutes or until they are firm enough to lift without breaking, then transfer to a wire rack to cool completely. The biscuits can be kept in an airtight tin for up to 5 days.

Some more ideas

• Instead of shaping the biscuits by hand, roll out the dough on a lightly floured surface to 5 mm (¼ in) thick and use shaped cutters to stamp out biscuits. Bake for 5–7 minutes.

• For oat and orange ginger biscuits, instead of all wholemeal flour use 45 g (1½ oz) plain wholemeal flour and 45 g (1½ oz) rolled oats. Add the grated zest of 1 orange with the melted mixture, and use 1–2 tbsp orange juice to bind the mixture into a soft dough. Roll into balls, shape and bake as in the main recipe.

• For fruity ginger biscuits, peel, core and coarsely grate 1 dessert apple, and add to the flour mixture with 55 g (2 oz) sultanas and the grated zest of 1 lemon. Shape and bake as in the main recipe.

Plus points

• Making your own biscuits means you can include some wholemeal flour and control the amount of fat and sugar you use. Commercial biscuits are often very sugary and may also be high in hydrogenated fats.

• Ginger is a traditional remedy for nausea and can sometimes ease morning sickness in pregnancy. It is also known as an aid to digestion and circulatory problems.

Each biscuit provides
kcal 90, **protein** 1 g, **fat** 4 g (of which saturated fat 2 g), **carbohydrate** 14 g (of which sugars 4 g), **fibre** 1 g

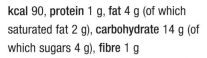

biscuits and bars

Five-star cookies

These nutty, moist cookies will cheer up mid-morning coffee or an afterschool snack. They are satisfying and packed full of healthy ingredients to restore flagging energy levels, without being too sweet. Barley flakes, which are slightly crisper than oatflakes, are available from most healthfood shops.

Makes 16 cookies

50 g (1¾ oz) hazelnuts, finely chopped
50 g (1¾ oz) sunflower seeds, finely chopped
50 g (1¾ oz) ready-to-eat dried apricots, finely chopped
50 g (1¾ oz) stoned dried dates, finely chopped
1 tbsp light muscovado sugar
50 g (1¾ oz) barley flakes
50 g (1¾ oz) self-raising wholemeal flour
½ tsp baking powder
2 tbsp sunflower oil
4 tbsp apple juice

Preparation time: 20 minutes
Cooking time: 10–15 minutes

1 Preheat the oven to 190ºC (375ºF, gas mark 5). Mix the chopped hazelnuts, sunflower seeds, apricots and dates together in a bowl. Add the sugar, barley flakes, flour and baking powder, and stir until all the ingredients are thoroughly combined.

2 Mix together the sunflower oil and apple juice, and pour over the dry mixture. Stir until the dry ingredients are moistened and clump together.

3 Scoop up a large teaspoonful of the mixture and, with dampened fingers, lightly press it together into a ball about the size of a large walnut. Then press it into a small, thick cookie about 5–6 cm (2–2½ in) in diameter. Neaten the edge with your fingers. Place on a large greased baking sheet. Repeat with the remaining mixture.

4 Bake the cookies for 10–15 minutes or until slightly risen and browned on top. Transfer to a wire rack and leave to cool. They can be kept in an airtight container for up to 4 days.

Some more ideas
• Use unsalted cashew nuts instead of hazelnuts.
• Use ready-to-eat dried peaches and figs instead of the apricots and dates.
• Substitute oatflakes or wheatflakes for the barley.

Plus points
• Sunflower seeds are a good source of the antioxidant vitamin E, which helps to protect cell membranes from damage by free radicals. Sunflower seeds are rich in polyunsaturated fats and also provide good amounts of vitamin B_1 and the minerals zinc, iron, phosphorus, selenium, magnesium and copper.
• Barley is thought to be the world's oldest cultivated grain. It is rich in starch and contains a type of dietary fibre called fructoligosaccharides (FOS), which is believed to stimulate the growth of friendly bacteria in the gut while inhibiting the growth of harmful bacteria.

Each cookie provides   Ⓥ
kcal 90, protein 2 g, fat 5 g (of which saturated fat 1 g), carbohydrate 9 g (of which sugars 4 g), fibre 1 g
✓   copper

Cranberry and almond biscotti

Biscotti means twice baked, a reference to the technique that gives these Italian biscuits their characteristically hard texture. Traditionally they are served after dinner, with a glass of Vin Santo for dipping, but they are also delicious with fresh fruit salad or a cup of coffee or tea at any time of day.

Makes 20 biscotti

50 g (1¾ oz) blanched almonds
1 large egg
85 g (3 oz) caster sugar
140 g (5 oz) plain flour
½ tsp baking powder
1 tsp ground cinnamon
55 g (2 oz) dried cranberries

Preparation time: 30 minutes
Cooking time: 30–40 minutes

Each biscotti provides

kcal 70, **protein** 1 g, **fat** 2 g (of which saturated fat 0 g), **carbohydrate** 12 g (of which sugars 6 g), **fibre** 0.5 g

1 Preheat the oven to 180°C (350°F, gas mark 4). Spread the almonds in a baking tin and toast them in the oven for about 10 minutes or until lightly browned. Set aside to cool.

2 Put the egg and sugar in a bowl and whisk with an electric mixer until very thick and pale; the mixture should be thick enough to leave a trail on the surface when you lift out the beaters. (If using a hand whisk or rotary beater, set the bowl over a pan of almost boiling water, making sure the water is not touching the base of the bowl.)

3 Sift the flour, baking powder and cinnamon onto a sheet of greaseproof paper, then sift the mixture again onto the whisked egg mixture. Using a large metal spoon, carefully fold the sifted mixture into the egg mixture, then stir in the toasted almonds and cranberries to make a stiff dough.

4 Spoon the dough onto a greased baking tray and, with floured hands, form it into a neat brick shape about 25 x 6 x 2 cm (10 x 2½ x ¾ in). Bake for 20–25 minutes or until golden brown. Leave to cool on the baking tray for 5 minutes, then transfer to a board.

5 Using a serrated bread knife, cut the brick across, slightly on the diagonal, into 20 slices. Arrange the slices flat on the baking tray and return to the oven. Bake for 10–15 minutes or until golden brown. Cool on the baking tray for about 5 minutes, then transfer to a wire rack and cool completely. The biscotti can be kept in an airtight tin for up to 2 weeks.

Some more ideas

• Substitute dried cherries or sultanas for the cranberries.
• For a stronger almond flavour, use ½ tsp pure almond extract instead of cinnamon.
• To make chocolate biscotti, replace the cranberries with 55 g (2 oz) coarsely chopped good dark chocolate (at least 70% cocoa solids). Add 1 tsp pure vanilla extract when you whisk the egg and sugar.

Plus points

• Almonds provide a good source of protein and also contain several vitamins and minerals, including vitamin E, several of the B-group vitamins, copper, zinc, iron, magnesium and phosphorus. They are a particularly useful source of calcium for people on dairy-free diets.
• Both fresh and dried cranberries are a good source of vitamin C.

biscuits and bars

Double chocolate chunk and nut cookies

These American-style cookies are simply irresistible eaten while still warm and the chocolate chunks are still soft and melting. Macadamia nuts, with their buttery flavour, add a crunchy texture, but can be omitted if you prefer. Like the chocolate, the nuts should be kept in fairly large pieces.

Makes 12 cookies

115 g (4 oz) unsalted butter, at room
   temperature
85 g (3 oz) light muscovado sugar
½ tsp pure vanilla extract
1 egg, beaten
85 g (3 oz) self-raising white flour
55 g (2 oz) plain wholemeal flour
20 g (¾ oz) cocoa powder
¼ tsp baking powder
¼ tsp salt
115 g (4 oz) good dark chocolate (at least
   70% cocoa solids), roughly chopped
55 g (2 oz) macadamia nuts, roughly chopped
3 tbsp semi-skimmed milk

Preparation time: 20 minutes
Cooking time: 15 minutes

Each cookie provides Ⓥ
kcal 240, **protein** 3 g, **fat** 15 g (of which
saturated fat 8 g), **carbohydrate** 22 g (of
which sugars 13 g), **fibre** 1 g

✓   A, copper

1 Preheat the oven to 190°C (375°F, gas mark 5). Line 2 baking sheets with baking parchment.

2 Beat the butter with the sugar and vanilla extract in a large bowl until light and fluffy. Gradually add the egg, beating well after each addition.

3 Sift the white and wholemeal flours, cocoa powder, baking powder and salt over the creamed mixture, tipping in any bran left in the sieve. Add the chocolate, nuts and milk, and mix everything together.

4 Place tablespoonfuls of the mixture on the prepared baking sheets, arranging the cookies well apart so there is space for them to spread during baking. Flatten the cookies slightly with the back of a fork, then bake for about 15 minutes or until they feel soft and springy.

5 Leave on the baking sheets for a few minutes, then transfer to a wire rack. Serve while still slightly warm or leave until cold. The cookies can be kept in an airtight container for up to 5 days.

Some more ideas

● Use walnuts or pecan nuts instead of macadamia nuts.

● For cherry and almond cookies, use plain white flour instead of the cocoa powder, and substitute 55 g (2 oz) dried sour cherries and 55 g (2 oz) flaked almonds for the chocolate chunks and macadamia nuts. If you want a pronounced almond flavour, use ¼ tsp pure almond extract instead of the vanilla.

Plus points

● Plain chocolate is a good source of copper and provides useful amounts of iron. The scientific name of the cocoa bean tree is Theobroma cacao, which means 'the food of the gods'. Casanova was reputed to drink hot chocolate before his nightly conquests – in fact, he was said to prefer chocolate to champagne.

● Butter contains useful amounts of the important fat-soluble vitamins A and D. Vitamin A is essential for healthy vision and skin, while vitamin D is needed for the formation of strong, healthy bones.

Orange and sesame flapjacks

Flapjacks are universally popular, and the light and fruity version here will appeal to the whole family. It's quick to mix, and not long in the oven. Serve the flapjacks with fresh fruit or yogurt for a speedy breakfast, in place of porridge, or enjoy them as a coffee-break or afterschool energy booster.

Makes 9 square flapjacks

2 tbsp sesame seeds
55 g (2 oz) unsalted butter
4 tbsp golden syrup
2 tbsp light muscovado sugar
grated zest of 1 orange
120 ml (4 fl oz) orange juice
250 g (8½ oz) rolled oats

Preparation time: 10 minutes
Cooking time: 20–25 minutes

1 Preheat the oven to 200°C (400°F, gas mark 6). Toast the sesame seeds in a small dry frying pan for a few minutes or until golden, then tip out onto a plate and leave to cool.

2 Place the butter, golden syrup, sugar, and orange zest and juice in a large saucepan and stir over a low heat for about 2 minutes or until the sugar has dissolved. Remove from the heat.

3 Add the sesame seeds and rolled oats to the melted mixture and stir until the oats are well moistened. Pour the mixture into a greased 19 cm (7½ in) square shallow cake tin and press down evenly with the back of a spoon. Bake for 20–25 minutes or until golden brown on top and firm to the touch.

4 Leave to cool in the tin for about 5 minutes, then cut the mixture into 9 squares. Leave the flapjacks in place for a further 10 minutes or until they are quite firm. Remove from the tin with a palette knife and leave to cool on a wire rack. They can be kept in an airtight container for up to 2 days.

Some more ideas

● For honey and banana flapjacks, use 3 tbsp clear honey instead of the golden syrup, and the grated zest and juice of 1 large lemon instead of the orange. Add 1 diced banana to the mixture with the oats.

● For apricot and apple flapjacks, add 100 g (3½ oz) chopped ready-to-eat dried apricots and 2 peeled, cored and diced dessert apples with the oats. Omit the sesame seeds.

Each flapjack provides Ⓥ

kcal 215, **protein** 4 g, **fat** 10 g (of which saturated fat 4 g), **carbohydrate** 30 g (of which sugars 10 g), **fibre** 2 g

✓   B₁, C, folate, copper, iron, zinc

Plus points

● Rolled oats are whole oat grains that have simply been husked and then rolled to flatten, and thus contain all of the nutrients of the whole grain.

● Sesame seeds provide calcium, which is essential for healthy bones and teeth, as well as vitamin E, an antioxidant that helps to protect against cancer.

biscuits and bars

Cereal bars

Naturally sweet and moist, these make a great addition to a packed lunch. They are also a good way of getting the family to try some more unusual grains and seeds, and add new healthy ingredients to the diet.

Makes 14 bars

2 tbsp sunflower seeds

2 tbsp pumpkin seeds

2 tbsp linseeds

2 bananas, about 300 g (10½ oz) in total, weighed with their skins on

100 g (3½ oz) unsalted butter

3 tbsp golden syrup

50 g (1¾ oz) millet flakes

100 g (3½ oz) rolled oats

100 g (3½ oz) stoned dried dates, roughly chopped

Preparation time: 25 minutes

Cooking time: 30 minutes

1 Preheat the oven to 180°C (350°F, gas mark 4). Grease a 28 x 18 x 4 cm (11 x 7 x 1½ in) cake tin and line the bottom with baking parchment. Roughly chop the sunflower seeds, pumpkin seeds and linseeds. Peel and roughly mash the bananas.

2 Melt the butter in a saucepan and stir in the golden syrup. Add the chopped seeds and mashed bananas, together with the millet flakes, rolled oats and dates. Mix together well, then spoon the mixture into the prepared tin and level the surface.

3 Bake for about 30 minutes or until golden brown. Leave to cool in the tin for 5 minutes, then mark into 14 bars and leave to cool completely. The bars can be kept in an airtight tin for up to 2 days.

Some more ideas

• Instead of dates, use chopped ready-to-eat dried apricots or prunes or a mixture of chopped dried fruits.

• Replace the millet flakes with plain flour, either white or wholemeal.

• The cereal bars can be frozen and will keep for 2 months. Wrap them individually in freezer wrap or foil. Then, if you simply pack a frozen bar into a plastic container along with wrapped sandwiches, it will have thawed by lunchtime.

Plus points

• Naturally occurring fruit sugars found in bananas and dates are released more slowly into the blood stream by the body, giving a more sustained energy boost. Extrinsic or 'added' sugars (such as table sugar, honey and golden syrup), on the other hand, are quickly absorbed and burnt up by the body.

• Seeds are a rich source of protein and are particularly valuable for those following a vegetarian diet.

• Linseeds are an excellent source of omega-3 fatty acids, essential for brain and eye development in the foetus.

Each bar provides

kcal 160, **protein** 3 g, **fat** 10 g (of which saturated fat 4 g), **carbohydrate** 17 g (of which sugars 8 g), **fibre** 1 g

✓ A, B$_1$, B$_6$, E, copper, zinc

biscuits and bars

Fig rolls

Here's a classic – a crisp, shortbread paste wrapped around a rich fig filling. The natural sweetness and full flavour of dried figs need little embellishment other than lemon juice to add a zesty tang.

Makes 20 biscuits

115 g (4 oz) plain white flour

115 g (4 oz) plain wholemeal flour

150 g (5½ oz) unsalted butter, cut into small pieces

65 g (2¼ oz) light muscovado sugar

1 tsp pure vanilla extract

2 egg yolks

250 g (8½ oz) ready-to-eat dried figs, finely chopped

2 tbsp lemon juice

Preparation time: 35 minutes, plus 30 minutes chilling

Cooking time: 12–15 minutes

Each biscuit provides

kcal 130, **protein** 2 g, **fat** 7 g (of which saturated fat 4 g), **carbohydrate** 17 g (of which sugars 10 g), **fibre** 1.5 g

✓　A, B$_6$

1 Sift the white and wholemeal flours into a mixing bowl, tipping in any bran left in the sieve. Rub in the butter with your fingertips until the mixture resembles breadcrumbs.

2 Add the sugar, vanilla extract and egg yolks, and mix to a firm dough, adding 1–2 tsp water if necessary to bind. (Alternatively, blend the flours and butter in a food processor, then add the sugar, vanilla and egg yolks, and blend briefly to make a dough.) Wrap in cling film and chill for 30 minutes.

3 Put the figs in a small, heavy-based saucepan with 6 tbsp water. Bring to the boil, then reduce the heat, cover and simmer gently for 3–5 minutes or until the figs have plumped up slightly and absorbed the water. Transfer to a bowl and mash lightly with a fork to break up the pieces. Add the lemon juice and stir, then leave to cool.

4 Preheat the oven to 190°C (375°F, gas mark 5). Roll out the dough on a lightly floured surface to a 50 x 15 cm (20 x 6 in) rectangle. Cut the dough rectangle in half lengthways to make 2 strips.

5 Spoon half the fig purée evenly along each strip, near one of the long sides. Bring the opposite long side up and over the filling, to form a 'log' shape, and press the edges of the dough together to seal.

6 Flatten each of the logs slightly. Using a sharp knife, cut each log across into 10 biscuits and transfer to a greased baking sheet. Prick each biscuit with a fork or score with a sharp knife. Bake for 12–15 minutes or until slightly darkened in colour.

7 Transfer the biscuits to a wire rack to cool. They can be kept in an airtight container for 2–3 days (don't mix them with other biscuits or the shortbread might go soft).

Another idea

● To make cherry and apple rolls, gently simmer 100 g (3½ oz) dried cherries in a saucepan with 5 tbsp water and 1 cored and finely chopped dessert apple until the water is absorbed. Use instead of the fig filling.

Plus point

● Dried fruits are a useful source of iron in the diet, particularly for those eating little or no red meat. In addition to iron, dried figs also offer good amounts of calcium. Just 3 dried figs (55 g/2 oz) will provide around 20% of the RNI (recommended daily amount) of calcium and 17% of the RNI of iron for a woman aged 19–50.

Fudgy brownies

Most people's ideal brownie is one that is moist in the centre, almost gooey, and with a rich, deep chocolate flavour. This recipe uses both chocolate and cocoa powder, which gives the brownies plenty of chocolate flavour, and also contains muscovado sugar to help produce the desired fudgy texture.

Makes 16 brownies

85 g (3 oz) good dark chocolate (at least 70% cocoa solids)

100 g (3½ oz) unsalted butter

125 g (4½ oz) caster sugar

100 g (3½ oz) light muscovado sugar

1 tsp pure vanilla extract

2 whole eggs and 1 egg yolk, at room temperature, beaten together

100 g (3½ oz) plain flour

3 tbsp cocoa powder

Preparation time: 15 minutes

Cooking time: 30 minutes

Each brownie provides

kcal 170, **protein** 2 g, **fat** 8 g (of which saturated fat 5 g), **carbohydrate** 23 g (of which sugars 18 g), **fibre** 0 g

✓ A, B$_{12}$

1 Preheat the oven to 180°C (350°F, gas mark 4). Grease an 18 cm (7 in) square shallow cake tin and line the bottom with baking parchment.

2 Break up the chocolate and put it in a heatproof bowl with the butter. Set the bowl over a pan of simmering water, making sure the water is not touching the base of the bowl. Leave until melted, then remove the bowl from the heat and set aside to cool.

3 Stir the caster and muscovado sugars into the chocolate mixture together with the vanilla extract. Gradually beat in the eggs and yolk. Sift over the flour and cocoa powder, and stir until evenly blended. Do not overmix.

4 Pour the mixture into the prepared tin. Bake for about 30 minutes or until risen but still slightly soft in the middle – a skewer inserted in the centre should come out with a few moist crumbs sticking to it. The surface will look cracked. It is important not to overcook or the brownies will be dry.

5 Leave in the tin for 5 minutes, then turn out onto a wire rack and leave to cool. When cold, peel off the lining paper and cut into 16 squares. If possible, wrap the brownies in foil and leave until the next day before eating. They can be kept like this for 3–4 days.

Some more ideas

● Fold in 55 g (2 oz) coarsely chopped pecan nuts after adding the flour mixture.

● For blondies, which are similar fudgy-textured cakes made without chocolate, melt the butter with 225 g (8 oz) light muscovado sugar in a saucepan over a moderate heat, stirring often. When the sugar has dissolved, simmer for 1 minute, but do not boil. Leave to cool for 10 minutes, then stir in the vanilla extract, 1 egg and 1 egg yolk. Fold in 140 g (5 oz) plain flour until just combined. Do not overmix. Pour into the prepared cake tin and bake for 20–25 minutes, testing as in the main recipe.

Plus points

● These are a healthier version of a traditionally high-fat favourite. The fat content is reduced by substituting cocoa powder for some of the chocolate. Cocoa powder contains 5 times as much iron as chocolate.

● Although eggs contain cholesterol, eating them normally has little effect on blood cholesterol levels. As eggs are a valuable source of protein, vitamins and minerals, they are a nutritious food to include in a healthy, well-balanced diet.

biscuits and bars

Basic and Savoury Breads

Super ways to boost carbohydrate intake

BREAD HAS A REPUTATION for being time-consuming and difficult to make, but nothing could be further from the truth. Once you have discovered the magic of baking bread – the mysterious rising process, the wonderful yeasty aromas, the fun of making different shapes – and produced your own home-baked loaves, you'll realise that most commercial bread just can't compete. You can use all kinds of flours and grains, nutritious oils, energy-packed nuts and seeds, and even fruit and vegetables, to ensure that every bite contributes to a healthy diet.

Basic loaf

This recipe makes a very good basic loaf, but it is also infinitely flexible. You can make any number of breads with it, just by using different types of flour or adding herbs, nuts, cheese, olives, seeds, dried fruit and berries, or you can shape it into rolls. You don't even need a loaf tin as the bread is baked on a baking tray.

Makes 1 large round loaf (cuts into about 12 slices)

340 g (12 oz) strong white (bread) flour
340 g (12 oz) strong wholemeal (bread) flour, preferably stoneground, plus a little extra to sprinkle
1 tsp salt
1 sachet easy-blend dried yeast, about 7 g
450 ml (15 fl oz) tepid water

Preparation time: 25 minutes, plus about 2 hours rising
Cooking time: 35 minutes

Each slice provides ⓥ

kcal 180, **protein** 6 g, **fat** 1 g (of which saturated fat 0 g), **carbohydrate** 40 g (of which sugars 1 g), **fibre** 3 g

✓✓	B₁, B₆, selenium
✓	niacin, copper, iron, zinc

1 Sift the white and wholemeal flours and salt into a large bowl, tipping in any bran left in the sieve. Stir in the dried yeast, then make a well in the centre and pour in the tepid water. Using your hands, gradually draw the flour into the water, mixing well to make a dough.

2 Gather the dough into a ball that feels firm and leaves the sides of the bowl clean; if necessary, add a little more flour or a little more water.

3 Turn the dough out onto a lightly floured work surface and knead for about 10 minutes or until smooth and elastic. Put the dough into a large, lightly greased bowl and cover with cling film. Leave to rise in a warm place for about 1 hour or until doubled in size.

4 Turn out the risen dough onto a floured work surface and knock it back with your knuckles. Gently knead the dough into a neat ball shape, then set it on a large greased baking sheet. Cover with a damp tea-towel and leave to rise in a warm place for 1 hour or until doubled in size again.

5 Towards the end of the rising time, preheat the oven to 220°C (425°F, gas mark 7). Uncover the loaf and sprinkle with a little flour, then make 4 slashes across the top using a small serrated knife. Bake for 35 minutes or until the bread sounds hollow when tapped on the base.

6 Transfer the loaf to a wire rack and cool completely before slicing. It can be kept for up to 5 days.

Plus points

• This is a fat-free loaf with plenty of fibre from the wholemeal flour. The wholemeal flour also provides B vitamins, magnesium, zinc, selenium, iron, copper and phosphorus.
• Stoneground flour is milled by traditional methods, which keep the wheat grains cool and thus preserve almost all the nutrients in the whole grain.

basic and savoury breads

Some more ideas

• For a white loaf, use 675 g (1½ lb) strong white (bread) flour and omit the wholemeal flour. For a loaf with plenty of texture, use 675 g (1½ lb) strong wholemeal (bread) flour and omit the white flour.

• For extra calcium, mix the dough with tepid semi-skimmed milk instead of water, or use a mixture of milk and water.

• To make a tin loaf, after the first rising shape the dough (see page 25) and place in a greased 900 g (2 lb) loaf tin. Leave to rise until doubled in size, then bake as in the main recipe.

• For rolls, after the first rising divide the dough into 20 equal pieces. For round rolls, shape each piece into a rough ball, then roll it under your cupped hand on the work surface to neaten. For an oval roll, shape each piece into a ball, flatten slightly, then mould to an oval with your hands and make a good crease down the centre with the side of your little finger.

Multigrain seeded loaf

Serve this nutty-textured loaf very fresh, cut into wedges. It's good with a hearty bowl of soup or cheese and pickles. The mix of seeds can be varied to your own taste, or you can use just one kind.

Makes 1 round loaf (cuts into 8 wedges)

300 g (10½ oz) strong white (bread) flour
200 g (7 oz) strong wholemeal (bread) flour
100 g (3½ oz) buckwheat flour
75 g (2½ oz) polenta
2 tsp salt
1 sachet easy-blend dried yeast, about 7 g
1 tsp light muscovado sugar
3 tbsp sunflower seeds
2 tbsp pumpkin seeds
2 tbsp linseeds
2 tbsp sunflower oil
450 ml (15 fl oz) tepid water
a little semi-skimmed milk to glaze

Preparation time: 30 minutes, plus about
    2 hours rising
Cooking time: 30–35 minutes

Each wedge provides Ⓥ

kcal 390, **protein** 11 g, **fat** 11 g (of which saturated fat 1 g), **carbohydrate** 65 g (of which sugars 2 g), **fibre** 5 g

✓✓✓	E
✓✓	B₁, B₆, folate, niacin, copper, selenium, zinc
✓	calcium, iron

1 Sift the white, wholemeal and buckwheat flours into a large bowl, tipping in any bran left in the sieve. Stir in the polenta, salt, yeast and sugar.

2 Mix together all the seeds, then set aside 1 tbsp for the topping. Stir the rest into the flour mixture.

3 Make a well in the centre of the dry ingredients and pour in the oil and most of the water. Gradually work the dry ingredients into the liquid to make a soft dough, adding the rest of the water as needed. Turn the dough out onto a work surface and knead for 10 minutes or until smooth and elastic.

4 Place the dough in a large, lightly greased bowl and cover with a damp tea-towel. Leave in a warm place for 1½ hours or until doubled in size.

5 Turn the risen dough out onto a lightly floured surface and knock it back with your knuckles, then knead firmly for a few minutes. Shape into a 20 cm (8 in) round and place on a lightly greased baking sheet. Cover with oiled cling film and leave to rise for 20–30 minutes or until well risen and springy to the touch.

6 Towards the end of the rising time, preheat the oven to 230°C (450°F, gas mark 8). Uncover the loaf and, using a sharp knife, cut deeply to mark it into 8 wedges. Brush with milk and sprinkle with the reserved seeds.

7 Bake for 15 minutes, then reduce the oven temperature to 200°C (400°F, gas mark 6). Bake for a further 15–20 minutes or until the loaf is golden brown and sounds hollow when tapped on the base. Cool on a wire rack. This is best eaten on the day it is made.

Some more ideas

• Shape the dough into a 'bubble loaf'. Roll it into about 8 balls and pack them together in a round shape, just touching, on the baking sheet. After baking they can be pulled apart and served as rolls.

• Instead of polenta, use medium oatmeal, and replace the seeds with 3 tbsp rolled oats, 2 tbsp poppy seeds and 2 tbsp sesame seeds.

Plus points

• Seeds are packed with essential fatty acids. Linseed, for instance, is one of the best sources of omega-3 fats, while sunflower seeds are an excellent source of omega-6.

• Pumpkin seeds are one of the richest vegetarian sources of zinc, a mineral that is essential for the functioning of the immune system. They are a good source of protein and unsaturated fat and a useful source of iron, magnesium and fibre.

Quick wholemeal bread

With only one rising and no kneading, this bread couldn't be simpler to make. It is based on the famous 'Grant loaf', invented in the 1940s by Doris Grant, who wanted to devise a quick, nutritious loaf that everyone could make at home. With its dense, moist texture, it is a filling bread that makes excellent toast.

Makes 1 large loaf (cuts into about 14 slices)

450 g (1 lb) strong wholemeal (bread) flour, preferably stoneground
1 tsp salt
2 tsp easy-blend dried yeast
1 tsp light muscovado sugar or clear honey
450 ml (15 fl oz) tepid water
1 tbsp plain white flour to dust

Preparation time: 10 minutes, plus about 30 minutes rising
Cooking time: 30–40 minutes

Each slice provides Ⓥ

kcal 100, **protein** 4 g, **fat** 1 g (of which saturated fat 0 g), **carbohydrate** 21 g (of which sugars 1 g), **fibre** 3 g

✓✓	selenium
✓	B₁, B₆, folate, niacin, copper, zinc

1 Lightly grease a 900 g (2 lb) loaf tin or line with baking parchment. Set it aside in a warm place while you make the dough.

2 Sift the flour and salt into a large mixing bowl, tipping in any bran left in the sieve. Stir in the yeast and make a well in the centre. Stir the sugar or honey into the tepid water, then add to the well in the dry ingredients.

3 Mix together, then beat vigorously with your hand (or with a wooden spoon) for about 2 minutes or until the dough comes away from the side of the bowl; it will be very soft and sticky.

4 Pour the dough into the prepared tin, cover with a damp tea-towel and leave in a warm place for about 30 minutes or until the dough has risen almost to the top of the tin.

5 Towards the end of the rising time, preheat the oven to 200°C (400°F, gas mark 6). Uncover the tin and dust the top of the loaf evenly with the white flour. Bake for 30–40 minutes or until well risen and brown. It should feel light and sound hollow when turned out of the tin and tapped on the base.

6 Turn out the loaf and, if necessary, return it to the oven for 5 minutes to crisp the sides and base. Leave on a wire rack to cool. It can be kept for up to 5 days.

Some more ideas

• For a light malted wholemeal loaf, replace the wholemeal flour with 200 g (7 oz) malted brown flour, 225 g (8 oz) strong white (bread) flour and 30 g (1 oz) fine oatmeal. Before baking, glaze with beaten egg and sprinkle over 2 tbsp kibbled wheat.

• Instead of wholemeal flour, use spelt flour to make a lighter-textured, slightly sweet and nutty-flavoured loaf. Spelt flour is richer in minerals than ordinary wholemeal flour. It is high in protein, but low in gluten, which makes it a suitable wheat flour-substitute for those who are gluten intolerant.

• To make 2 small loaves, divide the dough between two 450 g (1 lb) loaf tins and bake for 30–35 minutes.

Plus points

• Wholemeal bread provides more B-group vitamins and dietary fibre than bread made from refined white flour.
• Yeast is particularly rich in folate and contains traces of several other B vitamins.

Focaccia

This light Italian flat bread is prepared from a soft dough enriched with olive oil. Extra olive oil is traditionally sprinkled over the dough before baking – sometimes in generous quantities – but this recipe uses just enough to give a good texture and flavour. Focaccia makes an ideal accompaniment to Italian meats, cheeses and salads.

Makes 1 round, flat bread (serves 8)

450 g (1 lb) strong white (bread) flour
1 tsp salt
1 sachet easy-blend dried yeast, about 7 g
4 tbsp extra virgin olive oil
300 ml (10 fl oz) tepid water
½ tsp coarse sea salt

Preparation time: 15 minutes, plus about
    45 minutes rising
Cooking time: 15 minutes

Each serving provides Ⓥ
kcal 240, **protein** 5 g, **fat** 6 g (of which saturated fat 1 g), **carbohydrate** 44 g (of which sugars 1 g), **fibre** 2 g

✓   B₁, calcium

1 Put the flour into a large bowl and stir in the salt and yeast. Make a well in the centre and pour in 3 tbsp of the olive oil and the tepid water. Gradually mix the flour into the oil and water, using a wooden spoon at first, then by hand, to make a soft, slightly sticky dough.

2 Turn the dough out onto a floured surface and knead for about 10 minutes or until smooth and elastic. Keep the dough moving by turning, punching and folding it to prevent it from sticking. Sprinkle the surface with a little extra flour if necessary, but try not to add too much as this will make the dough dry.

3 Shape the dough into a ball and slap it onto a greased baking sheet, then roll it out (or push it out with your hands) into a round about 21 cm (8½ in) in diameter and 2 cm (¾ in) thick. Cover loosely with a clean tea-towel, tucking the ends under the baking sheet, and leave in a warm place for about 45 minutes or until the dough has doubled in thickness.

4 Towards the end of the rising time, preheat the oven to 230ºC (450ºF, gas mark 8). Uncover the bread. Pour a little hand-hot water into a cup, then dip your fingers into the water and press into the risen dough to make deep dents

all over the top; wet your fingers each time, to leave the top of the loaf moist. Brush the remaining 1 tbsp olive oil over the bread and sprinkle with the coarse salt.

5 Bake the focaccia for about 15 minutes or until golden brown. Transfer to a wire rack to cool for 15 minutes, then wrap it in a clean tea-towel to soften the crust. Serve warm or allow to cool completely. The bread can be kept in a polythene bag for up to 2 days.

Plus points

• Olive oil is high in monounsaturated fat, which may help to lower blood cholesterol levels.

• Although focaccia has slightly more fat than other types of bread, it has a moist texture and so can be eaten plain, without spreading with butter or other fat.

basic and savoury breads

Some more ideas

● To make individual focaccia, divide the dough into 8 portions. Press each portion out into a round about 10 cm (4 in) in diameter. These small breads will rise in 30–45 minutes and bake in 10–15 minutes.

● A variety of ingredients can be sprinkled over the focaccia before baking. Try fennel or dill seeds, chopped fresh or dried oregano, finely chopped onion and/or garlic, or chopped black or green olives.

● For olive focaccia, stone and chop 8 black olives and add to the dough with the olive oil and water. Sprinkle 1 tsp finely chopped fresh rosemary over the focaccia before making the dents on the surface with your fingers.

● For thyme and garlic focaccia, add 1 tbsp chopped fresh thyme to the dough with the oil and water, and sprinkle over 2 finely chopped garlic cloves before making the dents.

● For sun-dried tomato focaccia, add 4 finely chopped sun-dried tomatoes to the dough with the oil and water. Before serving, sprinkle with some shredded fresh basil.

Light rye bread

Rye flour is lower in gluten than wheat, so it produces a close-textured, moist loaf. Caraway seeds are a traditional seasoning, complementing the nutty flavour of rye to make an excellent bread that goes well with fish – particularly smoked mackerel, grilled kippers and pickled herrings – and soft cheeses.

Makes 1 small loaf (cuts into about 24 thin slices)

300 g (10½ oz) rye flour
100 g (3½ oz) strong white (bread) flour
½ tsp salt
1 tsp caster sugar
1 sachet easy-blend dried yeast, about 7 g
2 tsp caraway seeds
2 tbsp extra virgin olive oil
200 ml (7 fl oz) tepid water

Preparation time: 20 minutes, plus about 1 hour rising
Cooking time: 40–45 minutes

Each slice provides ⓥ
kcal 65, **protein** 1.5 g, **fat** 1 g (of which saturated fat 0 g), **carbohydrate** 13 g (of which sugars 0 g), **fibre** 1.5 g

1 Sift the rye flour, white flour, salt and sugar into a bowl, and stir in the yeast and caraway seeds. Stir the olive oil into the tepid water, then pour this over the flour mixture. Mix the ingredients together with a wooden spoon at first, then with your hand, to make a stiff, but sticky and slightly grainy dough.

2 Turn the dough out onto a floured work surface and knead for about 10 minutes or until smooth. The dough should be very firm. Shape it into an oval loaf about 18 cm (7 in) long, and place it on a greased baking sheet. Cover loosely with cling film and leave to rise in a warm place for about 1 hour or until almost doubled in size. It will be slightly cracked on top.

3 Towards the end of the rising time, preheat the oven to 200°C (400°F, gas mark 6). Uncover the loaf and bake for 40–45 minutes or until it is lightly browned and sounds hollow when tapped on the base.

4 Transfer to a wire rack and leave to cool. Once cold, place the loaf in a polythene bag and leave overnight (this allows the crust to soften). After this, the loaf can be kept for up to 2 days.

Some more ideas
● To make dark rye bread, stir 2 tbsp molasses or black treacle into the water with the olive oil.
● Substitute wholemeal flour for the white flour.
● For a lighter loaf, use 200 g (7 oz) rye flour and 200 g (7 oz) strong white (bread) flour.
● Cumin or fennel seeds also taste good in rye bread. Toast 1 tbsp of the seeds in a small, heavy-based frying pan over a moderate heat for 1–2 minutes or until they are aromatic. Remove from the heat at once and leave to cool. Add to the flour instead of the caraway seeds.
● For a mixed seed rye bread, replace the caraway seeds with a mixture of 2 tbsp poppy seeds, 2 tbsp toasted sunflower seeds, 1 tbsp toasted fennel seeds and 1 tbsp sesame seeds.
● For orange and caraway rye bread, add the grated zest of 1 large orange and 2 tbsp light muscovado sugar to the flour with the seeds, and substitute sunflower oil for the olive oil.

Plus points
● Making a variety of breads from different types of flour means that there is always an interesting loaf to complement a meal. This will help to increase the intake of starchy carbohydrates.
● Caraway seeds are said to stimulate the production of saliva and aid digestion.

Mediterranean spiral loaf

This unusual loaf is made with a mixture of white and wholemeal flours, plus fennel seeds for a subtle, aniseed flavour. The dough is rolled up round a roasted vegetable filling, so when the loaf is sliced there is a colourful spiral running through it. It makes a great addition to a lunchbox – there's no need to make sandwiches!

basic and savoury breads

Makes 1 loaf (cuts into about 8 slices)

250 g (8½ oz) strong white (bread) flour
200 g (7 oz) strong wholemeal (bread) flour
1 tsp salt
1 sachet easy-blend dried yeast, about 7 g
¼ tsp caster sugar
1 tbsp fennel seeds
300 ml (10 fl oz) semi-skimmed milk
30 g (1 oz) butter
2 red or yellow peppers, halved and seeded
3 tbsp sun-dried tomato paste
½ small red onion, thinly sliced
3 tbsp freshly grated Parmesan cheese
1 tsp extra virgin olive oil

Preparation time: 35 minutes, plus 1½–2 hours rising
Cooking time: 35–40 minutes

Each slice provides   Ⓥ
kcal 280, protein 11 g, fat 7 g (of which saturated fat 4 g), carbohydrate 45 g (of which sugars 6 g), fibre 4 g

✓✓✓	A, C
✓✓	B₁, B₆, calcium, selenium
✓	B₁₂, E, folate, niacin, copper, iron, zinc

1 Sift the white and wholemeal flours and the salt into a bowl, tipping in any bran left in the sieve. Stir in the yeast, sugar and fennel seeds. Make a well in the centre.

2 Gently heat the milk with the butter until the butter melts. Cool slightly until tepid, then pour into the well in the flour mixture. Gradually draw the flour into the liquid to make a soft dough.

3 Turn out onto a lightly floured work surface and knead for 10 minutes or until the dough is smooth and no longer sticky. Shape into a ball, place in a greased bowl and cover with a damp tea-towel. Leave to rise in a warm place for 1–1½ hours or until doubled in size.

4 Meanwhile, preheat the grill to high. Grill the pepper halves, skin side up, until slightly blackened. Place in a polythene bag and leave to cool, then peel off the skins. Slice the peppers into long strips.

5 Turn out the dough onto a lightly floured surface and knock back, then knead briefly until smooth. Roll out into a 20 x 33 cm (8 x 13 in) rectangle. Spread with the sun-dried tomato paste, leaving a 1 cm (½ in) border clear all round, then top with the pepper strips and red onion slices, in one layer. Sprinkle 2 tbsp of the Parmesan cheese evenly over the top.

6 Roll up the dough firmly from a short side, like a Swiss roll. Tuck the ends under and place in a lightly oiled 900 g (2 lb) loaf tin. Cover and leave in a warm place for 30 minutes or until risen and springy to the touch.

7 Towards the end of the rising time, preheat the oven to 230ºC (450ºF, gas mark 8). Uncover the loaf and cut several slashes across the top with a sharp knife. Brush with the olive oil and sprinkle with the remaining 1 tbsp Parmesan. Bake for 15 minutes, then reduce the oven temperature to 200ºC (400ºF, gas mark 6). Bake for a further 20–25 minutes or until the loaf is risen and golden brown and sounds hollow when turned out and tapped on the base.

8 Turn out onto a wire rack and leave to cool. This loaf is best eaten on the day it is made.

Plus point
• Red peppers offer an impressive arsenal of disease-fighting compounds. In addition to being an excellent source of vitamin C and beta-carotene, they contain 2 other important phytochemicals, lutein and zeaxanthin. These are believed to help protect against the eye disease, age-related macular degeneration.

Some more ideas

• To make individual spiral rolls, roll out the dough into a rectangle as in the main recipe, then cut into 8 smaller rectangles. Fill and roll them up, place on a greased baking sheet and bake for 15–20 minutes or until risen and golden brown.

• To make a garlic and herb spiral loaf, roll out the dough as in the main recipe and spread it with 2–3 crushed garlic cloves instead of the tomato paste. Replace the peppers and red onion with 2 tbsp each of chopped fresh basil, parsley, chives and spring onions. Instead of Parmesan, sprinkle the loaf with a little coarse sea salt before baking.

Potato bread

Made in the traditional way, with freshly mashed potato, this soft, light bread has a lovely rich flavour and moist texture. It's very good thinly sliced and used for delicate sandwiches, or toasted and spread lightly with honey. The potato greatly improves the keeping qualities of the loaf.

Makes 2 small loaves (each cuts into 14 slices)

400 g (14 oz) floury potatoes, scrubbed and cut into large pieces
700 g (1 lb 9 oz) strong white (bread) flour
1 tsp salt
1 sachet easy-blend dried yeast, about 7 g
1 tbsp molasses

Preparation time: 45 minutes, plus about 1 hour rising
Cooking time: 40–45 minutes

1 Put the potatoes in a pan of boiling water and simmer for 15 minutes or until tender. Drain, reserving the cooking water. When the potatoes are cool enough to handle, peel off the skins. Mash the potatoes until smooth, then leave to cool.

2 Sift 600 g (1 lb 5 oz) of the flour into a large bowl with the salt. Add the mashed potatoes and rub them into the flour with your fingertips until well blended. Add the yeast to the mixture and stir it in well.

3 Measure 300 ml (10 fl oz) of the potato cooking water, which should be tepid. Add the molasses and stir until dissolved. Pour this mixture into the flour mixture and mix well to combine. It is easiest to do this with your hands. Work in as much of the remaining flour as needed to give a soft but not sticky dough.

4 Turn out onto a floured surface and knead for 5–10 minutes or until smooth and quite elastic. Put the dough in a large greased bowl and cover with a tea-towel. Leave to rise in a warm place for about 40 minutes or until increased by about one and a half times in size.

5 Turn out the dough onto the floured surface again and knock it back, then knead for about 3 minutes. Divide the dough in half and shape each piece into a loaf (see page 25). Place the loaves in 2 well-greased 450 g (1 lb) loaf tins. Cover again with the tea-towel and leave to rise in a warm place for about 20 minutes.

6 Towards the end of the rising time, preheat the oven to 180°C (350°F, gas mark 4). Uncover the loaves and bake for 40–45 minutes or until they are well risen and brown, and sound hollow when tipped out of their tins and tapped on the base. Turn them out onto a wire rack to cool. This bread can be kept for up to a week.

Each slice provides Ⓥ

kcal 195, **protein** 6 g, **fat** 1 g (of which saturated fat 0 g), **carbohydrate** 43 g (of which sugars 1 g), **fibre** 2 g

| ✓✓ | selenium |
| ✓ | B₁, B₆, calcium |

Plus points
● Cooking potatoes in their skins preserves the nutrients that lie just beneath the skin.
● Using the potato cooking water in the dough not only increases the potato flavour, it retains the water-soluble vitamins (C) and minerals that will have seeped out into the liquid during cooking.

Some more ideas

● To make griddled onion and rosemary potato bread, knead 1 tsp chopped fresh rosemary into the dough at the end of step 3. Cut 1 red onion into slices 1 cm (½ in) thick. Brush lightly with extra virgin olive oil and cook on a preheated ridged cast-iron grill pan or under a very hot grill until tender and browned on both sides, turning once. Remove from the heat and chop coarsely. Allow to cool slightly, then knead into the dough before dividing it in half and shaping into loaves.

● To make a hearty potato bread, replace half the white flour with wholemeal flour.

● For an Eastern European potato bread, replace 200 g (7 oz) of the white flour with rye flour, and add 1 tsp lightly crushed caraway seeds with the yeast.

Gluten-free bread

This golden, crusty loaf has a delicious, moist, close-textured interior. The ingredients are readily available from healthfood shops and the recipe is simplicity itself. Yeast gives a traditional flavour, while bicarbonate of soda and cream of tartar help to make the bread rise.

Makes 1 loaf (cuts into about 15 slices)
200 g (7 oz) brown rice flour
200 g (7 oz) potato flour
100 g (3½ oz) soya flour
1 tsp salt
1 sachet easy-blend dried yeast, about 7 g
1½ tsp honey
1 tsp extra virgin olive oil
400 ml (14 fl oz) hand-hot water
1 tsp bicarbonate of soda
2 tsp cream of tartar

Preparation time: 10 minutes, plus about
   30 minutes rising
Cooking time: 25–30 minutes

Each slice provides
kcal 130, **protein** 4 g, **fat** 2 g (of which
saturated fat 0.2 g), **carbohydrate** 23 g (of
which sugars 1.5 g), **fibre** 2 g

✓   folate, copper

1 Sift the rice, potato and soya flours into a large bowl with the salt. Remove about one-quarter of the mixture and set aside. Stir the yeast into the mixture left in the bowl and make a well in the centre.

2 Add the honey and olive oil to the well, together with the hand-hot water. Stir the dry ingredients into the liquid to make a smooth, thick batter.

3 Cover the bowl with cling film and leave in a warm place for 30 minutes to allow the yeast to become active. Towards the end of this time, preheat the oven to 200°C (400°F, gas mark 6).

4 Mix the bicarbonate of soda and cream of tartar with the reserved flour mixture, then sift it on top of the yeast batter. Stir gently until combined; the mixture will look foamy. Transfer it to a well-greased non-stick 900 g (2 lb) loaf tin.

5 Bake for 25–30 minutes or until firm, crisp and golden brown. Turn out onto a wire rack to cool. This bread can be kept for up to 2 days and is very good toasted.

Some more ideas
● For a dark gluten-free loaf, use just 50 g (1¾ oz) soya flour and replace the potato flour with 200 g (7 oz) buckwheat flour. This loaf has a dark crust and dark, moist crumb, with a close texture.

● For a delicious corn-flavoured gluten-free loaf, substitute 200 g (7 oz) cornmeal, 200 g (7 oz) cornflour and 100 g (3½ oz) buckwheat flour for the brown rice, potato and soya flours. Use 360 ml (12 fl oz) hand-hot water. This loaf has a paler crust and a level, slightly cracked top.

● For a golden gluten-free loaf, substitute 200 g (7 oz) cornmeal or polenta and 200 g (7 oz) ground rice for the brown rice, potato and soya flours. Use 360 ml (12 fl oz) hand-hot water. This loaf has a light-golden, crazed top and a slightly grainy texture.

Plus points
● This loaf is suitable not only for gluten-free diets but also for wheat-free ones.

● A mixture of 1 part bicarbonate of soda and 2 parts cream of tartar makes a good alternative to commercial baking powder, which may contain traces of gluten.

basic and savoury breads

Bagels

These little bread rings, Jewish in origin, are delicious teamed with savoury fillings such as smoked salmon and a soft cheese, or egg and salad. The double cooking method – first by briefly poaching in boiling water, then baking – gives bagels their unique soft crumb and slightly chewy crust.

Makes 12 bagels

450 g (1 lb) strong white (bread) flour
1½ tsp salt
1 sachet easy-blend dried yeast, about 7 g
3 eggs
1 tsp clear honey
2 tsp sunflower oil
200 ml (7 fl oz) tepid water

Preparation time: 35 minutes, plus about
   1 hour rising
Cooking time: 15 minutes

Each bagel provides ⓥ
kcal 160, **protein** 6 g, **fat** 3 g (of which saturated fat 0.5 g), **carbohydrate** 29 g (of which sugars 1 g), **fibre** 1 g

✓✓	selenium
✓	B₁, B₁₂

1 Put the flour into a large mixing bowl and stir in the salt and yeast. Make a well in the centre.

2 Lightly whisk 2 of the eggs with the honey and oil, and pour into the well in the flour. Add the water and mix to a soft dough.

3 Turn out onto a lightly floured surface and knead for 10 minutes or until smooth and elastic. Place the dough in a large greased bowl, cover with a damp tea-towel and leave to rise in a warm place for 40 minutes or until doubled in size.

4 Turn out the dough onto the floured work surface and knead it lightly, then divide it into 12 equal pieces. Form each into a 20 cm (8 in) long sausage, then shape it into a ring. Dampen the ends with a little water, slightly overlap them and gently pinch together to seal.

5 Arrange the bagels on a lightly oiled baking sheet, cover with oiled cling film and leave to rise in a warm place for 20 minutes or until they are slightly puffy.

6 Preheat the oven to 200°C (400°F, gas mark 6). Bring a large pan of lightly salted water to the boil. Drop the bagels into the water, one at a time, and poach for 20 seconds. Lift out with a large draining spoon and return to the baking sheet.

7 Lightly beat the remaining egg and brush it over the bagels to glaze. Bake for 14–15 minutes or until well risen and golden brown. Transfer to a wire rack to cool. The bagels can be kept in an airtight container for up to 3 days.

Plus points

● Enriching the bagel dough with eggs increases the protein, iron and zinc content, as well as adding vitamins A, D and E and some of those in the B group.

● Serving the bagels with a vitamin-C rich fruit, or including a vitamin-C rich salad in the bagel filling, will help the body to absorb the iron provided by the bagels.

Some more ideas

• For cinnamon and raisin bagels, soak 85 g (3 oz) raisins in 3 tbsp orange juice for about 2 hours or until the juice has been absorbed. Make the dough as in the main recipe, but reduce the salt to 1 tsp and add 30 g (1 oz)

caster sugar and 1 tsp ground cinnamon with the flour. Mix in the raisins with the water.

• For rye bagels, substitute 170 g (6 oz) rye flour for 170 g (6 oz) of the white flour. Stir in 1 tsp caraway seeds with the yeast, and use molasses instead of honey.

• The bagels can be finished with a variety of toppings. After brushing them with the egg glaze, sprinkle with sesame, poppy, nigella or caraway seeds, or try sprinkling them with 1 finely chopped small onion tossed in 1 tbsp extra virgin olive oil.

Pitta breads

These pitta breads are delicious served freshly baked, warm from the oven. They make a good accompaniment to soups, dips and pâtés or they can be left to cool, then split and filled: try goat's cheese with roasted vegetables and red onion rings; grilled meat and vegetables; or hummus and a crunchy mixed salad.

Makes 10 breads

450 g (1 lb) strong white (bread) flour
1 tsp salt
½ tsp caster sugar
1 sachet easy-blend dried yeast, about 7 g
300 ml (10 fl oz) tepid water, or as needed

Preparation time: 30 minutes, plus 1½–2 hours rising
Cooking time: 8–10 minutes

Each bread provides Ⓥ
kcal 155, **protein** 4 g, **fat** 0.5 g (of which saturated fat 0 g), **carbohydrate** 35 g (of which sugars 1 g), **fibre** 1.5 g

✓ B₁, folate, calcium

1 Sift the flour and salt into a bowl, then stir in the sugar and yeast. Make a well in the centre and mix in enough water to make a soft dough.

2 Turn the dough out onto a lightly floured surface and knead for about 10 minutes or until it is smooth and elastic. Place in a lightly greased bowl, cover with a tea-towel and leave to rise in a warm place for 1–1½ hours or until the dough has doubled in size.

3 Turn the risen dough onto the lightly floured surface and knock it back, then knead for 2–3 minutes. Divide it into 10 pieces and shape each one into a ball. Roll out each ball to an oval about 5 mm (¼ in) thick. Leave on the floured surface to rise at room temperature for about 30 minutes.

4 Towards the end of the rising time, preheat the oven to 230°C (450°F, gas mark 8). Place 3 non-stick baking sheets (or 3 floured baking sheets) in the oven to heat for about 5 minutes. Place the pitta breads on the hot baking sheets and bake for 8–10 minutes or until firm and golden brown.

5 Transfer to a wire rack to cool. Serve warm or reheat under the grill, or in the toaster, as required. Pitta breads are best eaten on the day they are made, but they can be kept, wrapped in foil, for 1–2 days.

Some more ideas

● Substitute wholemeal flour for half the white flour.

● For seeded pitta breads, brush the dough ovals with water, then sprinkle with sesame or other seeds before baking. Alternatively, knead 2 tbsp seeds into the dough in step 2.

● For herb pitta breads, knead 1 tbsp chopped fresh rosemary or 2 tbsp chopped fresh basil into the dough in step 2.

Plus points

● White flour provides calcium, a mineral that is essential for healthy bones and teeth. Calcium is also important for normal functioning of nerve impulses and it aids blood clotting.

● These pitta breads contain no saturated fat and almost no fat of any kind, making them an excellent healthy choice for a bread to serve with cheese, meat or other foods that are higher in fat.

Pizza alla napoletana

A home-made pizza is vastly superior in flavour to shop-bought versions, and making your own pizza base – just a bread dough enriched with olive oil – is easy to do. Once you get the hang of it, you can add pizza toppings to order. The topping here, with tomatoes, mozzarella, anchovies and olives, is a classic from Naples.

Serves 4

340 g (12 oz) strong white (bread) flour

½ tsp salt

1 sachet easy-blend dried yeast, about 7 g

200 ml (7 fl oz) tepid water

2 tbsp extra virgin olive oil

Napoletana topping

2 tbsp extra virgin olive oil

1 small onion, finely chopped

2 garlic cloves, crushed

2 cans chopped tomatoes, about 400 g each

½ tsp caster sugar

small handful of fresh basil leaves, torn into pieces

150 g (5½ oz) mozzarella cheese, thinly sliced

8 anchovy fillets, halved lengthways

8 black olives, stoned and halved

salt and pepper

Preparation time: 45 minutes, plus 1–1½ hours rising

Cooking time: 20–25 minutes

Each serving provides   Ⓥ

kcal 560, **protein** 23 g, **fat** 22 g (of which saturated fat 6 g), **carbohydrate** 72 g (of which sugars 9 g), **fibre** 4 g

✓✓✓	B₆, B₁₂, calcium
✓✓	A, B₁, C, E, niacin, selenium
✓	B₂, folate, iron, zinc

1 Put the flour into a bowl and stir in the salt and yeast. Make a well in the centre and add the water and olive oil. Mix with a round-bladed knife until the mixture forms a soft dough, adding a little more water if it feels too dry.

2 Turn the dough out onto a lightly floured surface and knead for about 10 minutes or until smooth and elastic. Place the dough in a large, lightly greased bowl, cover with cling film and leave to rise in a warm place for 1–1½ hours or until doubled in size.

3 Meanwhile, make the topping. Heat the olive oil in a saucepan, add the onion and garlic, and cook gently, stirring, for 3 minutes or until softened. Add the tomatoes with their juice, the sugar, and salt and pepper to taste, and bring to the boil. Leave the mixture to bubble, stirring frequently, until reduced by about half to make a thick sauce. Remove from the heat and leave to cool.

4 Turn out the risen dough onto the lightly floured surface and knock it back, then knead very lightly. Roll or press out to a round about 30 cm (12 in) in diameter and transfer to a greased baking sheet.

5 Stir the basil into the tomato sauce. Spread the sauce over the pizza base to within 1 cm (½ in) of the edge. Arrange the mozzarella, anchovies and olives over the top, then leave the pizza in a warm place for about 15 minutes. Meanwhile, preheat the oven to 220°C (425°F, gas mark 7).

6 Bake the pizza for 20–25 minutes or until the crust has risen and is golden and the cheese has melted. Cut into wedges and serve warm.

Plus points

● Canned tomatoes are a rich source of the phytochemical lycopene (other good sources include pink grapefruit, watermelon and guava). Lycopene can help to protect against several types of cancer and heart disease.

● Allicin, the compound that gives garlic its characteristic smell and taste, acts as a powerful antibiotic. It also has antiviral and antifungal properties. Recent studies suggest that garlic may also help to protect against cancer of the stomach and colon.

Some more ideas

• To make roasted vegetable pizza, cut 2 small red onions into wedges; cut 1 red and 1 yellow pepper into chunks; and thinly slice ½ small aubergine (about 150 g/5½ oz). Toss the vegetables with 4 tbsp extra virgin olive oil in a roasting tin, then roast in an oven preheated to 200°C (400°F, gas mark 6) for 30 minutes or until soft and just beginning to char. Arrange the vegetables on the tomato sauce in place of the mozzarella and anchovies, and scatter over the olives. After baking, sprinkle with 30 g (1 oz) Parmesan cheese, cut into shavings.

• To make spinach, mushroom and chorizo pizza, put 200 g (7 oz) baby spinach leaves in a saucepan, cover and cook for 1–2 minutes or until just wilted; drain well. Fry 200 g (7 oz) sliced chestnut mushrooms in 15 g (½ oz) butter until their liquid has evaporated and they are just starting to colour. Arrange the spinach and mushrooms on the tomato sauce in place of the mozzarella, anchovies and olives. Scatter over 30 g (1 oz) thinly sliced chorizo sausage and 2 tbsp pine nuts, then rise and bake.

Sourdough bread

Instead of commercial yeast, deliciously tangy sourdough bread is made with a 'starter' which uses the yeasts that occur naturally in the atmosphere and on flour. Despite the time needed to 'grow' the starter, it is not a difficult bread to make, and leftover starter can continue to be 'fed', to make more sourdough loaves.

Makes 1 large round loaf (cuts into about 20 slices)

Starter

100 g (3½ oz) strong white (bread) flour, preferably unbleached organic flour

100 ml (3½ fl oz) tepid water, preferably spring water

To 'feed'

200–300 g (7–10½ oz) strong white (bread) flour, preferably unbleached organic flour

tepid water, preferably spring water

Dough

500 g (1 lb 2 oz) strong white (bread) flour, preferably unbleached organic flour

1 tsp salt

240 ml (8 fl oz) tepid water, preferably spring water, or as needed

Preparation time: 40 minutes, plus 4–6 days for the starter to develop and 5–14 hours rising

Baking time: 35 minutes

Each slice provides ⓥ

kcal 120, **protein** 3 g, **fat** 0 g (of which saturated fat 0 g), **carbohydrate** 27 g (of which sugars 0.5 g), **fibre** 1 g

1 For the starter, stir the flour and water together in a bowl to make a sticky paste. Cover with a damp tea-towel (not cling film) and leave on the kitchen counter for 2 days, dampening the tea-towel again as needed to keep it moist. If after 2 days the mixture looks bubbly and has a milky smell, you can proceed to the first feed. (It may take up to 4 days to reach this stage.) If there are patches of mould or the paste smells sour or bad, throw it away and start again with a new batch of starter.

2 To feed, stir in 100 g (3½ oz) flour and enough tepid water to make a soft, paste-like dough. Cover the bowl and leave as before for 24 hours. At this point the starter will look very active and bubbly. Stir well, then discard half the starter. Add another 100 g (3½ oz) flour and enough tepid water to make a dough, as before. Cover again and leave for 12 hours. If the starter looks very bubbly and lively, it is ready to use. If it seems only slightly bubbly, give it one more feed and wait 6 hours.

3 For the dough, mix the flour with the salt in a large bowl and make a well in the centre. Weigh out 200 g (7 oz) of the sourdough starter and mix it with the tepid water, then pour it into the well in the flour. Gradually work the flour into the liquid mixture to make a

soft dough. You may need to add a little more water if the dough feels dry or crumbly, or more flour if it sticks to your hands or the bowl.

4 Turn the dough out onto a floured work surface and knead for about 10 minutes or until very pliable. Return it to the cleaned bowl, cover with a damp tea-towel and leave to rise in a warm place for 3–8 hours or until doubled in size. Rising time depends on the room temperature and on the strength of your starter. (A new starter will give a slower rise and less volume than one that is well established.)

5 Turn out the risen dough onto a floured work surface and knock it back with your knuckles to its original size. Shape the dough into a ball and set it in a basket or colander lined with a heavily floured linen tea-towel. Cover with a damp tea-towel and leave to rise for 2–6 hours or until doubled in size.

6 Towards the end of the rising time, preheat the oven to 220°C (425°F, gas mark 7). Invert the loaf onto a large greased baking sheet and quickly slash the top with a sharp knife. Bake for about 35 minutes or until the bread sounds hollow when tapped on the base.

7 Transfer the bread to a wire rack and leave to cool. It can be kept for up to 5 days, and is wonderful toasted.

Some more ideas

● Leftover sourdough starter can be stored in an airtight container in the fridge. Before using it to make another loaf, bring it back to room temperature, then feed it once as in the main recipe and leave for about 6 hours. Each time you make a loaf, you will have leftover starter. This can be kept in the fridge, feeding it every 4 days to keep it alive, and will improve in flavour. Any starter you do not need or want can be discarded, or given to a friend.

● Instead of spring water you can use water that has been filtered, boiled and cooled.

● To make a French-style sourdough bread, replace 50 g (1¾ oz) of the white flour with strong wholemeal (bread) flour.

● To make a heavier, German-style sourdough bread, replace half the white flour with rye flour.

Plus point

● Sourdough starters can last for decades, and seem to be resistant to contamination. This may be due to an antibiotic action similar to that of the moulds in cheeses such as Stilton and Roquefort.

Soft flour tortillas

Tortillas, either made from wheat flour or cornmeal, are the basic bread that accompanies almost every meal in Mexico. These flour tortillas are easy to make and they have a multitude of uses – serve with meals in place of bread, make wraps with sandwich fillings, or roll round a savoury mixture, sprinkle with cheese and bake.

Makes 10 small tortillas

225 g (8 oz) plain flour
55 g (2 oz) lard, cut into small pieces
1 tsp salt
120 ml (4 fl oz) hand-hot water

Preparation time: 25 minutes, plus about 1 hour chilling
Cooking time: about 10 minutes

1 Sift the flour into a mixing bowl. Add the lard and rub it in with your fingertips until thoroughly incorporated. Stir in the salt, then add the water and stir well to form a smooth dough.

2 Turn out onto a lightly floured work surface and knead for 2–3 minutes. Wrap the dough in cling film and chill for about 1 hour.

3 Divide the dough into 10 pieces and shape each one into a ball. Roll out each ball on the lightly floured surface, keeping an even round shape, to make a paper-thin disc about 15 cm (6 in) in diameter. As they are rolled, stack them up, interleaved with sheets of greaseproof paper.

4 Heat a griddle or cast-iron frying pan over a moderate heat until very hot. Cook the tortillas, one or two at a time (depending on the size of your pan), for 20–30 seconds on each side or until bubbles appear on the surface and they are lightly browned. As the tortillas are cooked, stack them up on a plate and keep covered with a clean tea-towel. Serve warm, preferably straight from the griddle.

Some more ideas

● To reheat leftover tortillas for serving, wrap the stack in foil and put into a preheated 180°C (350°F, gas mark 4) oven for 10–15 minutes. Alternatively, they can be heated individually on a moderately hot griddle for 10–15 seconds on each side.

● For heartier tortillas, replace half the white flour with wholemeal flour.

● To make tomato herb tortillas, add 1 tsp tomato purée and ½ tsp each chopped fresh basil and thyme with the water.

● For spicy tortillas, add typical Mexican spices, such as a pinch each of ground cumin, coriander and cinnamon, to the flour.

Each tortilla provides
kcal 125, **protein** 2 g, **fat** 6 g (of which saturated fat 2 g), **carbohydrate** 17 g (of which sugars 0.3 g), **fibre** 0 g

✓   B₁

Plus point
● Lard, which is rendered pure pork fat, is a traditional ingredient in tortillas. It has an unhealthy image, but weight for weight, lard contains less saturated fat than butter. In 100 g (3½ oz) lard the total fat content is 99 g, of which 40 g is saturated; in the same weight of butter, total fat is 81 g of which 54 g is saturated.

basic and savoury breads

Naan breads

Naan is an Indian flat bread, traditionally baked on the sides of a clay tandoor oven. The familiar teardrop shape develops when the bread stretches as it hangs inside the oven. This simple recipe produces fabulous naan under the grill – beautifully light and soft. Best of all, they are quick and fun to make.

Makes 4 breads

2 tsp sunflower oil
250 g (8½ oz) plain flour
¼ tsp salt
½ tsp bicarbonate of soda
170 g (6 oz) Greek-style yogurt

Preparation time: 20 minutes
Cooking time: 3–4 minutes per naan

1 Cut out 4 pieces of foil, each about 28 x 20 cm (11 x 8 in), and brush them with the oil. Sift the flour, salt and bicarbonate of soda into a bowl. Add the yogurt and stir until thoroughly mixed to make a fairly soft dough. Turn out onto a lightly floured surface and knead for 5–7 minutes or until smooth.

2 Preheat the grill to high. Cut the dough into quarters. On the lightly floured surface, roll out one portion into an elongated oval, about 25 cm (10 in) long and 18 cm (7 in) wide across the middle. Lay the bread oval on one of the prepared pieces of foil. Repeat with the remaining portions of dough.

3 Place a naan, on its foil, under the grill, about 15–20 cm (6–8 in) away from the heat if possible. Cook until the bread bubbles up and browns slightly in places – this takes about 2 minutes, but watch it constantly to ensure that it does not overcook.

4 Turn the naan and cook the second side for 1–2 minutes or until firm and browned in places. Wrap the cooked naan in a tea-towel to keep hot while grilling the remaining breads. Serve hot or warm.

Some more ideas

● For coriander naan, add 4 tbsp chopped fresh coriander and 2 tbsp finely chopped spring onions with the yogurt.

● For garlic naan, add 1 finely chopped garlic clove with the yogurt.

● To make stuffed naan, heat 1 tbsp sunflower oil in a small saucepan and add the seeds from 2 green cardamom pods, 2 coarsely grated carrots and 2 finely chopped spring onions. Sprinkle 2 tbsp raisins on top and cover the pan. Cook over a low heat for 5 minutes, stirring occasionally. Set aside to cool. Divide this mixture into quarters. Roll out a portion of naan dough into an 18 cm (7 in) round. Place a portion of the carrot mixture on one side of the dough round and fold the other side over to make a half-moon shape. Gently press and roll out the filled dough into an oval shape, keeping the surface floured and turning the dough over once. Repeat with the remaining dough and filling. Grill the naan as in the main recipe.

Each bread provides

Ⓥ

kcal 275, **protein** 9 g, **fat** 6 g (of which saturated fat 2 g), **carbohydrate** 50 g (of which sugars 2 g), **fibre** 2 g

✓ B_1, B_2, B_6, E, calcium

Plus point

● The addition of yogurt increases the calcium content of the bread and adds useful amounts of phosphorus and vitamins B_2 and B_{12}. Calcium from dairy products such as yogurt is much more readily absorbed than calcium from other foods.

Irish soda bread

Quick and simple to make, freshly baked soda bread tastes terrific. In the version here it's made with half wholemeal flour to give it a delicious coarse texture and nutty flavour. It goes well with butter and jam for breakfast, or with soups and salads for lunch. Or wedges can be split for favourite sandwich fillings.

Serves 8

250 g (8½ oz) plain white flour

250 g (8½ oz) plain wholemeal flour, plus a little extra to sprinkle

1 tsp bicarbonate of soda

½ tsp salt

300 ml (10 fl oz) buttermilk

Preparation time: 10 minutes

Cooking time: 30 minutes

1 Preheat the oven to 200°C (400°F, gas mark 6). Sift the white and wholemeal flours, bicarbonate of soda and salt into a bowl, tipping in any bran left in the sieve.

2 Make a well in the centre and pour in the buttermilk. With a wooden spoon, gradually stir the flour into the buttermilk to form a soft dough. Bring the dough together with your hands, then turn it out onto a lightly floured work surface. Knead lightly and briefly until it forms a smooth ball.

3 Place the dough on a greased baking sheet and flatten it slightly to make a domed round loaf about 19 cm (7½ in) in diameter. Using a sharp knife, cut a deep cross in the top of the loaf, cutting about halfway down into the dough. Sprinkle a little extra wholemeal flour over the top.

4 Bake for about 30 minutes or until well risen and browned, and the bread sounds hollow when tapped on the base. (If it sounds moist and heavy, bake for a further 3–5 minutes and then test it again.)

5 Transfer to a wire rack and leave to cool completely. Serve the loaf on the day it is baked, as it becomes stale quickly, or toast it the following day.

Some more ideas

● If you can't find buttermilk, you can use semi-skimmed milk instead and add it with 1 tbsp lemon juice. Alternatively, use semi-skimmed milk and sift 2 tsp cream of tartar with the flour, bicarbonate of soda and salt.

● For herb soda bread, add 2 tbsp chopped parsley, 2 tbsp chopped fresh chives and 1 tbsp chopped fresh sage at the end of step 1.

● For caraway soda bread, add 1 tbsp caraway seeds at the end of step 1.

● To make fruited soda bread, add 100 g (3½ oz) sultanas or raisins, 50 g (1¾ oz) cut mixed peel and the grated zest of 1 lemon at the end of step 1.

Each serving provides   ⓥ

kcal 217, **protein** 8 g, **fat** 1.5 g (of which saturated fat 0.2 g), **carbohydrate** 46 g (of which sugars 3 g), **fibre** 4 g

✓✓ selenium, zinc

✓ B$_1$, B$_6$, folate, calcium, copper

Plus points

● Buttermilk provides useful amounts of vitamin B$_2$, calcium and phosphorus.

● Home-baked bread is delicious and inexpensive, and ideal for boosting the starchy carbohydrate content of any meal. Making your own bread also gives you control over the amount of salt you add, rather than eating commercial loaves which may have a high salt content.

Courgette and hazelnut twist

Based on a quick soda bread, this low-fat, savoury loaf has lots of healthy additions – grated courgette, toasted hazelnuts and bran. With gentle handling, it is easily shaped into an attractive twist. Cut it into generous slices and serve with soup or a hearty salad for a satisfying lunch.

Makes 1 loaf (cuts into 16 slices)

1 small, firm courgette, about 115 g (4 oz)

400 g (14 oz) plain flour, plus extra to sprinkle

2 tsp bicarbonate of soda

1 tsp salt

30 g (1 oz) bran

55 g (2 oz) toasted hazelnuts, roughly chopped

1 tbsp light muscovado sugar

1 plump garlic clove, finely chopped

1 tbsp sunflower oil

400 ml (14 fl oz) buttermilk, or as needed

Preparation time: 20 minutes

Cooking time: 25–30 minutes

Each serving provides

kcal 130, **protein** 4 g, **fat** 3 g (of which saturated fat 0.3 g), **carbohydrate** 22 g (of which sugars 3 g), **fibre** 2 g

✓   calcium, zinc

1 Preheat the oven to 200°C (400°F, gas mark 6). Coarsely grate the courgette (including the skin) and press it between several sheets of kitchen paper to absorb the excess moisture. Set aside.

2 Sift the flour, bicarbonate of soda and salt into a large bowl. Add the bran, chopped nuts, sugar and garlic, then stir in the grated courgette.

3 Drizzle over the oil and gently stir in with the buttermilk using a round-bladed knife. Stir just until the mixture is combined into a soft dough. Do not overmix or the bread will be tough. If there are any dry bits of flour in the bottom of the bowl, add a little more buttermilk.

4 Gently gather the dough together into a rough ball and turn it out onto a lightly floured work surface. Cut the dough in half, and knead each piece very briefly until smooth. With floured hands, very gently roll each piece of dough to make a rope that is about 30 cm (12 in) long.

5 Lay the ropes side by side on the work surface. Pinch the top ends together, then carefully twist the ropes round each other, and tuck under the bottom ends. Lift the twisted loaf onto a greased baking sheet and sprinkle over a little extra flour.

6 Bake for 25–30 minutes or until risen and golden. Transfer to a wire rack and leave to cool slightly before slicing. This bread is best eaten freshly baked, but can be kept for up to 2 days.

Some more ideas

• Replace half of the courgette with finely grated carrot.

• For a courgette, cheese and chive twist, omit the hazelnuts and garlic, and stir in 55 g (2 oz) grated Edam cheese and 3 tbsp snipped fresh chives. Sprinkle a little extra grated cheese over the top of the loaf before baking.

• Instead of shaping the dough into a twist, keep it in one piece and shape into a round or ball-shaped loaf.

Plus points

• Courgettes provide several B vitamins, with their tender skins containing the greatest concentration of these nutrients. The skin is also rich in beta-carotene.

• Hazelnuts are particularly rich in vitamin E. A powerful antioxidant, vitamin E also helps to keep the heart healthy by preventing the oxidation of LDL cholesterol. In addition, studies suggest that vitamin E may help to boost fertility in men by protecting the sperm cell membranes from free radical damage.

basic and savoury breads

Boston brown bread

Being steamed rather than baked, this mixed-grain bread has a soft crust and close texture. It gets its dark, rich colour and flavour from molasses. It was created by American settlers in the days before most homes had ovens.

Makes 1 loaf (cuts into about 12 slices)

225 g (8 oz) self-raising wholemeal flour

225 g (8 oz) rye flour

225 g (8 oz) cornmeal or polenta

2 tsp salt

2 tsp bicarbonate of soda

200 g (7 oz) raisins

150 ml (5 fl oz) blackstrap molasses

600 ml (1 pint) buttermilk

4 tbsp semi-skimmed milk

Preparation time: 30 minutes

Cooking time: 2¼ hours

Each slice provides Ⓥ

kcal 290, **protein** 8 g, **fat** 2 g (of which saturated fat 0.3 g), **carbohydrate** 63 g (of which sugars 22 g), **fibre** 4.5 g

✓✓	B₆
✓	B₁, B₂, niacin, copper, iron, potassium, selenium, zinc

1 To make this bread, you need a tall cylindrical tin with a solid base, or a clean, empty coffee can about 15 cm (6 in) in diameter and at least 18 cm (7 in) tall. It should have a capacity of at least 2.2 litres (4 pints). If using a coffee can, you may find the top has a lip, which would make it difficult to remove the bread after cooking. Either cut it off with a sharp tin opener; or cut off the base, cover the sharp edges with masking tape, and use the lidded end as the base. Lightly grease your tin and line the bottom with baking parchment.

2 Put the wholemeal and rye flours, cornmeal, salt, bicarbonate of soda and raisins in a bowl. Mix thoroughly, and make a well in the centre.

3 Combine the molasses, buttermilk and milk in a saucepan and heat, stirring, until barely warm. Pour into the well in the flour mixture and quickly stir together. Spoon into the prepared tin. Cover the top of the tin with a pleated piece of oiled greaseproof paper, then with a pleated piece of foil, and tie them on tightly with string.

4 Place the tin on a trivet in a large pan and pour in enough boiling water to come three-quarters of the way up the side of the tin. Cover the pan with a tight-fitting lid (if you don't have a pan that is deep enough, use a dome of foil to cover the pan instead of a lid).

Steam for 2¼ hours – the water should be just bubbling very gently. Check from time to time, and top up with more boiling water if needed.

5 Remove the tin from the water and allow the bread to cool in the tin for 10 minutes. Turn out onto a wire rack to cool completely.

6 To serve, cut across into rounds, then cut each round into halves or quarters, if liked. The bread can be kept, wrapped in greaseproof paper and then in foil, in a cool place for up to 4 days.

Plus points

● Blackstrap molasses is the most nutritious type of molasses. A by-product of sugar refining, it contains iron, calcium, copper, phosphorus, potassium, magnesium and zinc.

● Rye is an important cereal crop in parts of Central Europe, such as Russia and Germany, and in Scandinavia, and is the basis for those countries' traditional breads. Nutritious rye flour offers B vitamins, vitamin E, iron, copper, zinc and fibre.

Another idea

• Make Chicago pumpernickel bread, also known as black bread (the recipe was taken from Germany to America's Mid-West in the 19th century). You need 2 clean, empty 400 g fruit cans. Grease the cans and line the bottom with baking parchment. Mix together 55 g (2 oz) plain flour, 55 g (2 oz) rye flour, 55 g (2 oz) fine semolina, ¾ tsp baking powder, ½ tsp salt and ½ tsp ground mixed spice. Gently warm 4 tbsp blackstrap molasses with 240 ml (8 fl oz) buttermilk until combined. Add to the dry ingredients and mix thoroughly. Divide the mixture between the cans, then cover and steam for 2 hours.

Sweet and Fruity Breads

Tea-time loaves full of good things

ENRICHED WITH DRIED OR FRESH FRUIT, teabreads are very healthy sweet treats – they're made with less sugar, and have lots of nutritional benefits to offer. A fruity teabread is equally at home on the breakfast table or at tea-time, and can be served toasted or fresh from the oven. Whether you fancy a light, summery teabread bursting with fresh blackcurrants, a richly fruited, traditional Welsh bara brith or spicy teacakes, you'll find that sweet fruity breads represent home baking at its best – comforting, delicious to eat and made with the best ingredients.

Cinnamon raisin bread

This milk-enriched fruity loaf tastes good plain or can be served spread with a little honey or jam. It's also wonderful toasted for breakfast, when the gentle aroma of warm cinnamon makes a soothing start to the day.

Makes 1 large loaf (cuts into about 16 slices)

450 g (1 lb) strong wholemeal (bread) flour

1½ tsp salt

2 tsp ground cinnamon

1 sachet easy-blend dried yeast, about 7 g

115 g (4 oz) raisins

45 g (1½ oz) caster sugar

55 g (2 oz) unsalted butter

240 ml (8 fl oz) semi-skimmed milk, plus 1 tbsp to glaze

1 egg, lightly beaten

Preparation time: 20 minutes, plus about 1 hour rising

Cooking time: 30 minutes

Each slice provides

Ⓥ

kcal 156, **protein** 5 g, **fat** 4 g (of which saturated fat 2 g), **carbohydrate** 26 g (of which sugars 9 g), **fibre** 3 g

✓✓ selenium

✓ B₁, B₆, folate, niacin, copper, iron, zinc

1 Grease and lightly flour a 900 g (2 lb) loaf tin. Sift the flour, salt and cinnamon into a large mixing bowl, tipping in any bran left in the sieve. Stir in the yeast, raisins and sugar, and make a well in the centre.

2 Gently heat the butter and milk in a small saucepan until the butter has melted and the mixture is just tepid. Pour into the well in the dry ingredients and add the beaten egg. Mix together to make a soft dough.

3 Turn the dough out onto a lightly floured surface and knead for 10 minutes or until smooth and elastic. Shape the dough (see page 25) and place in the prepared tin. Cover with oiled cling film or a clean tea-towel and leave to rise in a warm place for about 1 hour or until doubled in size.

4 Towards the end of the rising time, preheat the oven to 220°C (425°F, gas mark 7). Uncover the loaf and brush with the milk to glaze. Bake for about 30 minutes or until it sounds hollow when removed from the tin and tapped on the base. Cover the loaf with foil towards the end of the cooking time if the top is browning too much.

5 Turn out onto a wire rack and leave to cool. The bread can be kept, wrapped in foil, for 2–3 days.

Some more ideas

• Vary the flavour of the loaf by using other dried fruit, such as chopped ready-to-eat dried apricots or luxury dried mixed fruits.

• Use the dough to make maple and pecan Chelsea buns. Omit the raisins and, after kneading, roll out the dough to a 23 cm (9 in) square. Beat together 30 g (1 oz) softened butter and 4 tbsp maple syrup, and spread over the dough. Scatter over 115 g (4 oz) finely chopped dried dates and 55 g (2 oz) chopped pecan nuts. Roll up the dough like a Swiss roll and slice across into 9 equal pieces. Arrange, cut side down, in 3 rows of 3 in a greased 18 cm (7 in) square cake tin. Cover with oiled cling film and leave to rise in a warm place for about 30 minutes. Brush the top with milk and sprinkle with 2 tsp demerara sugar. Bake in a preheated 200°C (400°F, gas mark 6) oven for 25 minutes or until well risen and lightly browned. Turn out onto a wire rack to cool before separating into buns. These can be kept in an airtight tin for up to 3 days.

Plus points

• Semi-skimmed milk and egg add protein and other nutrients to this loaf.

• Dried fruit, such as raisins, are a concentrated source of energy. Raisins are also a useful source of fibre and potassium.

Fruit and nut bread

This heavily fruited German-style loaf is good at tea-time, served thickly sliced, or lightly toasted and buttered for breakfast. It contains no added fat (the fat present comes from the nuts), but the dried fruits – a mixture of apricots, pears, prunes and figs – give it a rich, moist texture and good keeping qualities.

Makes 1 round loaf (cuts into about 10 slices)

400 g (14 oz) strong white (bread) flour
½ tsp salt
grated zest of ½ lemon
1 sachet easy-blend dried yeast, about 7 g
85 g (3 oz) ready-to-eat dried apricots, roughly chopped
85 g (3 oz) ready-to-eat dried pears, roughly chopped
85 g (3 oz) stoned ready-to-eat prunes, roughly chopped
50 g (1¾ oz) ready-to-eat dried figs, roughly chopped
50 g (1¾ oz) chopped mixed nuts, such as almonds, hazelnuts and cashews
250 ml (8½ fl oz) tepid water

Preparation time: 50 minutes, plus 2½–3 hours rising
Cooking time: 30–40 minutes

Each slice provides Ⓥ

kcal 220, **protein** 6 g, **fat** 3 g (of which saturated fat 0.2 g), **carbohydrate** 44 g (of which sugars 14 g), **fibre** 3.5 g

✓ B₁, B₆, E, folate, copper, iron, potassium, zinc

1 Mix the flour with the salt, lemon zest and yeast in a large bowl. Add the chopped fruits and nuts and mix in well. Stir in the tepid water and work the mixture with your hand to make a soft-textured, heavy dough.

2 Turn the dough out onto a lightly floured work surface and knead for 10 minutes or until it feels pliable. Place the dough in a lightly greased bowl, cover with a damp tea-towel and leave to rise in a warm place for 1½–2 hours or until doubled in size.

3 Turn the risen dough out onto the floured work surface and knock it back with your knuckles to return it to its original size. Gently knead the dough into a neat ball shape, then set it on a well-greased baking sheet. Cover with a damp tea-towel and leave to rise in a warm place for about 1 hour or until doubled in size.

4 Towards the end of the rising time, preheat the oven to 200°C (400°F, gas mark 6). Uncover the loaf and bake for 30–40 minutes or until it is nicely browned and sounds hollow when tapped on the base. Cover with foil if it is becoming too brown. Transfer to a wire rack and leave to cool. This bread can be kept for up to 5 days.

Another idea

● To make spicy fruit buns, add 2 tsp ground mixed spice and ¼ tsp freshly grated nutmeg to the flour with the salt. Omit the lemon zest. After the first rising, divide the dough into 12 equal portions. Shape them into neat balls (see Basic loaf, Some more ideas, page 107), then set them, spaced well apart, on greased baking sheets and leave to rise for about 45 minutes or until doubled in size. Bake for about 25 minutes or until they sound hollow when tapped on the base.

Plus points

● Ready-to-eat dried apricots are an excellent ingredient to have on hand in the storecupboard, as they are very nutritious – an excellent source of beta-carotene and a useful source of calcium – and versatile. They can be used in cakes, biscuits, teabreads and sweet yeasted breads, as well as making a delicious addition to breakfast cereals, stews and casseroles. And they are ideal for a healthy snack.

● Like all nuts, cashews are rich in protein and unsaturated fats. Cashews also provide useful amounts of iron, zinc and folate.

Malted sultana bread

This is a well-flavoured, pleasantly sweet bread with a moist texture and good keeping qualities. Slice it thickly and eat spread with a fruit purée or jam or soft fresh cheese.

Makes 1 small loaf (cuts into about 16 slices)

200 g (7 oz) strong wholemeal (bread) flour, preferably stoneground
150 g (5½ oz) strong white (bread) flour
½ tsp salt
1 tsp easy-blend dried yeast
3 tbsp malt extract
1 tbsp clear honey
200 ml (7 fl oz) tepid water
85 g (3 oz) sultanas

Preparation time: 20 minutes, plus about 2 hours rising
Cooking time: 35–40 minutes

Each slice provides Ⓥ
kcal 90, **protein** 3 g, **fat** 0.4 g (of which saturated fat 0 g), **carbohydrate** 20 g (of which sugars 5 g), **fibre** 1.5 g

✓ B₆, copper, selenium

1 Sift the wholemeal and white flours and the salt into a large bowl, tipping in any bran left in the sieve. Add the yeast and stir to mix, then make a well in the centre.

2 Stir the malt extract and honey into the tepid water, and pour into the well in the flour. Gradually work the flour into the liquids to make a soft but not sticky dough. Work in the sultanas.

3 Turn the dough out onto a lightly floured surface and knead for about 10 minutes or until very elastic. Place the dough in a greased bowl, cover with cling film and leave to rise in a warm place for about 1 hour or until doubled in size. Meanwhile, grease a 450 g (1 lb) loaf tin and line the bottom with baking parchment.

4 Turn the dough out onto the floured work surface again and knock it back with your knuckles. Gently shape the dough (see page 25) and put it into the prepared tin. Cover with a damp tea-towel and leave to rise in a warm place for 1 hour or until doubled in size.

5 Towards the end of the rising time, preheat the oven to 190ºC (375ºF, gas mark 5). Uncover the loaf and bake for 35–40 minutes or until it sounds hollow when turned out of the tin and tapped on the base. Turn it out onto a wire rack and leave to cool. The bread can be kept for up to 4 days.

Some more ideas

● For an attractive shiny finish, as soon as the bread comes out of the oven, brush the top with 2 tsp warmed clear honey.

● For a malted apple and sultana bread, add 1 medium-sized dessert apple, cored and diced, and 50 g (1¾ oz) lightly toasted and chopped almonds with the sultanas.

● Slightly stale malted sultana bread makes an excellent bread and butter pudding, and you don't need to add any extra dried fruit.

Plus points

● Malt extract is produced by soaking barley grains, then letting them germinate under controlled conditions so that the starch is converted into dextrin (a type of gum) and malt sugar (maltose). When added to baked goods, malt extract gives a distinctive taste and moist texture, and provides phosphorus and magnesium.

● Honey has been a much-prized source of sweetness since ancient times, and has been used throughout history to treat a range of different medical problems. In Chinese medicine, honey is believed to harmonise the liver, neutralise toxins and relieve pain.

sweet and fruity breads

Teacakes

These lightly spiced teacakes are packed full of nutritious dried fruit. They are simple to make and delicious served lightly toasted and spread with a little butter or jam at tea-time.

Makes 10 teacakes

225 g (8 oz) strong white (bread) flour
225 g (8 oz) strong wholemeal (bread) flour
1 tsp salt
55 g (2 oz) unsalted butter, cut into small
  pieces
1 sachet easy-blend dried yeast, about 7 g
30 g (1 oz) caster sugar
85 g (3 oz) sultanas
85 g (3 oz) currants
½ tsp ground cinnamon
300 ml (10 fl oz) tepid semi-skimmed milk,
  or as needed, plus extra for brushing

Preparation time: 25 minutes, plus 1½–3 hours
  rising
Cooking time: 10–15 minutes

Each teacake provides

kcal 255, **protein** 7 g, **fat** 5 g (of which
saturated fat 3 g), **carbohydrate** 47 g (of
which sugars 17 g), **fibre** 3 g

✓✓ B₁, selenium

✓   B₆, niacin, calcium, copper, iron, zinc

1 Sift the white and wholemeal flours and the salt into a large bowl, tipping in any bran left in the sieve. Rub in the butter, then stir in the yeast, sugar, sultanas, currants and cinnamon. Make a well in the centre and pour in the milk. Mix together, adding more milk as needed to make a soft dough.

2 Turn the dough out onto a lightly floured surface and knead for about 10 minutes or until smooth and elastic. Place in a lightly greased bowl, cover with a tea-towel and leave to rise in a warm place for 1–2 hours or until doubled in size.

3 Turn the dough out onto the lightly floured surface and knock it back. Knead for 2–3 minutes, then divide it into 10 equal pieces. Shape each piece into a round teacake (see Basic loaf, Some more ideas, page 107).

4 Place the teacakes on 2 greased baking sheets and cover with a tea-towel. Leave to rise in a warm place for 30–60 minutes or until puffy.

5 Towards the end of the rising time, preheat the oven to 220°C (425°F, gas mark 7). Uncover the teacakes and lightly brush the tops with milk. Bake for 10–15 minutes or until nicely browned, then transfer to a wire rack to cool. Serve warm, or split and toasted. These are best eaten on the day they are made, but can be kept for 1–2 days.

Some more ideas

• Instead of making individual teacakes, shape the dough into a large round and place on a greased baking sheet. Leave to rise again for 30–60 minutes, then bake for about 25 minutes.

• Use other dried fruit, such as raisins or chopped ready-to-eat dried pears, peaches or dates, instead of the sultanas and currants.

• Substitute freshly grated nutmeg or ground mixed spice for the cinnamon.

Plus points

• Dried fruit is low in fat and a useful source of fibre. Currants also provide magnesium, and sultanas offer potassium and iron.

• Combining wholemeal flour with white flour increases the fibre content of the teacakes and adds other valuable nutrients such as B vitamins and several minerals.

sweet and fruity breads

Bara brith

This favourite Welsh teabread – its name means 'speckled bread' – is usually made with a yeast dough by bakers and by a quick-mix method at home. Soaking the dried fruit in tea makes it very juicy, and produces a moist loaf with good keeping qualities. Serve it thickly sliced and lightly spread with butter or soft cheese.

Makes 1 large loaf (cuts into about 12 slices)

2 tea bags
330 ml (11 fl oz) boiling water
225 g (8 oz) mixed dried fruit
170 g (6 oz) self-raising white flour
170 g (6 oz) self-raising wholemeal flour
1 tsp baking powder
1 tsp ground mixed spice
55 g (2 oz) light muscovado sugar
1 egg, beaten

Preparation time: 10 minutes, plus at least
  5 hours soaking
Cooking time: 1¼ hours

Each slice provides   Ⓥ

kcal 170, **protein** 4 g, **fat** 1 g (of which saturated fat 0.2 g), **carbohydrate** 38 g (of which sugars 18 g), **fibre** 2 g

✓ B_1, B_6, copper, iron, selenium

---

1 Place the tea bags in a heatproof measuring jug and pour in the boiling water. Stir, then leave to infuse for 3–4 minutes. Put the dried fruit in a bowl. Remove the tea bags, squeezing them over the jug, and pour the tea over the fruit. Cover and set aside to soak for at least 5 hours or overnight.

2 Preheat the oven to 160°C (325°F, gas mark 3). Grease and line a 900 g (2 lb) loaf tin. Sift the white and wholemeal flours, baking powder and spice into a bowl, tipping in any bran left in the sieve. Stir in the sugar.

3 Pour in the soaked dried fruit, scraping in all the liquid from the bowl, and add the beaten egg. Lightly mix the egg and fruit together, then stir in the dry ingredients until thoroughly combined. The mixture should be soft enough to drop easily off the spoon. Add 2–3 tsp more hot water if needed.

4 Spoon the mixture into the prepared tin and spread it out evenly. Bake for about 1¼ hours or until the loaf is well risen and firm, cracked along the middle and browned on top. Cover loosely with foil for the last 20 minutes of baking if it is becoming too brown.

5 Leave to cool in the tin for about 5 minutes, then turn out onto a wire rack to cool completely. This teabread tastes particularly good if it is left for 1–2 days before eating. It can be kept, in a polythene bag in a cool place, for about 5 days.

Some more ideas

● Vary the flavour of the teabread by using different types of tea with just one kind of dried fruit. For example, try currants soaked in Earl Grey tea, or raisins soaked in rose-scented tea. Omit the mixed spice to avoid overpowering the delicate flavours of these teas.

● For bara brith with lime and jasmine, use jasmine tea bags and sultanas instead of mixed dried fruit. Replace the mixed spice with the grated zest of 1 lime, adding it to the dry ingredients with the sugar.

● For nutty bara brith, add 100 g (3½ oz) chopped walnuts with the sugar.

Plus point

● Most of the carbohydrate in dried fruit is in the form of sugars, but unlike refined sugar, dried fruit offers more than just sweetness – it is a valuable source of fibre and many other nutrients. Including a good amount of dried fruit in this teabread means that it contains far less sugar than bought teabreads. It is also very low in fat.

sweet and fruity breads

Blackcurrant teabread

Tart blackcurrants make an excellent summer teabread that is fruity without being too sweet, while mint adds a fresh, herbal note. If you have a glut of blackcurrants, make a few loaves and freeze for up to 2 months.

Makes 1 large loaf (cuts into about 12 slices)

340 g (12 oz) self-raising flour

1 tsp baking powder

50 g (1¾ oz) unsalted butter, cut into small pieces

100 g (3½ oz) light muscovado sugar

150 g (5½ oz) fresh blackcurrants

3 tbsp chopped fresh mint

150 ml (5 fl oz) orange juice, or as needed

Preparation time: 20 minutes

Cooking time: 1¼ hours

1 Preheat the oven to 180°C (350°F, gas mark 4). Grease and line a 900 g (2 lb) loaf tin. Sift the flour and baking powder into a bowl, then rub in the butter with your fingertips until the mixture resembles fine breadcrumbs. Stir in the sugar, and make a well in the centre.

2 Put the blackcurrants and mint into the well in the dry ingredients and pour in the orange juice. Gradually stir the dry ingredients into the liquid until everything is thoroughly combined. The mixture should be soft, so add 1–2 tbsp more orange juice if necessary.

3 Turn the mixture into the prepared tin and smooth the top. Bake for about 1¼ hours or until risen, brown and firm to the touch. If the loaf looks as though it is browning too much after about 50 minutes, place a piece of foil loosely over the top.

4 Leave the teabread to cool in the tin for 5 minutes, then turn it out onto a wire rack to cool completely. This teabread is best left overnight before serving, and can be kept in an airtight tin for up to 3 days.

Some more ideas

● Make blueberry teabread by substituting fresh blueberries for the blackcurrants.

● For cranberry pecan teabread – ideal for breakfast or tea-time over the festive Christmas season – substitute roughly chopped fresh cranberries for the blackcurrants. Instead of mint, add ½ tsp ground cinnamon, sifting it with the flour, and stir in 100 g (3½ oz) pecan nuts with the sugar.

Each slice provides

kcal 170, **protein** 3 g, **fat** 4 g (of which saturated fat 2 g), **carbohydrate** 32 g (of which sugars 11 g), **fibre** 1 g

✓✓ C

✓ B₁, potassium

Plus points

● Blackcurrants are an excellent source of vitamin C – weight for weight, they contain 4 times as much vitamin C as oranges. They also provide useful amounts of potassium, and are rich in a group of phytochemicals called bioflavonoids, which may help to protect against heart disease.

● The oils menthol, menthone and menthyl acetate, responsible for the characteristic flavour of mint, are believed to have powerful antiseptic properties. Naturopaths prescribe mint to help relieve toothache, stress headaches and digestive problems.

sweet and fruity breads

Spiced pumpkin teabread

Here's a delicious, richly coloured teabread that is moist enough to eat without butter. It makes a great addition to a healthy lunchbox, being rich in essential antioxidants, vitamins and minerals.

Makes 1 large loaf (cuts into about 12 slices)

340 g (12 oz) peeled pumpkin, diced

150 g (5½ oz) clear honey, plus 2 tsp to glaze

85 g (3 oz) sultanas

150 g (5½ oz) self-raising wholemeal flour

150 g (5½ oz) self-raising white flour

2 tsp ground allspice

150 g (5½ oz) unsalted butter, cut into small pieces

1 tbsp pumpkin seeds

Preparation time: 25 minutes

Cooking time: 50–60 minutes

1 Preheat the oven to 180°C (350°F, gas mark 4). Line a 900 g (2 lb) loaf tin with baking parchment.

2 Steam the pumpkin flesh, or cook it in just a little boiling water, for 10 minutes or until tender. Drain thoroughly, then mash with a potato masher until smooth. Add the honey and sultanas, and beat well.

3 Sift the wholemeal and white flours and the allspice into a bowl, tipping in any bran left in the sieve. Rub in the butter with your fingertips until the mixture resembles fine breadcrumbs.

4 Add the pumpkin mixture and beat well with a wooden spoon until evenly mixed. Tip the mixture into the prepared tin and smooth the surface. Sprinkle with the pumpkin seeds. Bake for 50–60 minutes or until the loaf is well risen, golden brown and firm to the touch.

5 Allow the loaf to cool in the tin for 10 minutes, then turn it out onto a wire rack. Gently brush with the 2 tsp honey while still warm. This teabread is best served slightly warm, or within a day of making.

Some more ideas

● Use butternut squash instead of pumpkin.

● For spiced pumpkin muffins, spoon the mixture into 12 paper muffin cases placed in the cups of a deep muffin tray. Sprinkle with the pumpkin seeds and bake for 20–25 minutes or until well risen and golden brown.

● To make date and walnut pumpkin loaf, instead of sultanas add 85 g (3 oz) chopped dried dates and 30 g (1 oz) chopped walnuts. Top the loaf with a few walnut halves instead of pumpkin seeds.

Plus points

● Pumpkin has a high water content, which makes it low in calories – just 15 kcal per 100 g (3½ oz). It provides carbohydrates, potassium, calcium and vitamins A and C. An excellent source of beta-carotene, pumpkin also provides several other antioxidants, including lutein and zeaxanthin.

● Steaming the pumpkin helps to preserve its content of water-soluble vitamin C. If you choose to boil it instead, be sure to use the minimum of water.

Each slice provides Ⓥ

kcal 240, **protein** 4 g, **fat** 11 g (of which saturated fat 7 g), **carbohydrate** 33 g (of which sugars 15 g), **fibre** 2 g

✓✓ A

✓ B$_1$, B$_6$, copper, selenium, zinc

A glossary of nutritional terms

Antioxidants These are compounds that help to protect the body's cells against the damaging effects of free radicals. Vitamins C and E, beta-carotene (the plant form of vitamin A) and the mineral selenium, together with many of the phytochemicals found in fruit and vegetables, all act as antioxidants.

Calorie A unit used to measure the energy value of food and the intake and use of energy by the body. The scientific definition of 1 calorie is the amount of heat required to raise the temperature of 1 gram of water by 1 degree Centigrade. This is such a small amount that in this country we tend to use the term kilocalories (abbreviated to *kcal*), which is equivalent to 1000 calories. Energy values can also be measured in kilojoules (kJ): 1 kcal = 4.2 kJ.

A person's energy (calorie) requirement varies depending on his or her age, sex and level of activity. The estimated average daily energy requirements are:

Age (years)	Female (kcal)	Male (kcal)
1–3	1165	1230
4–6	1545	1715
7–10	1740	1970
11–14	1845	2220
15–18	2110	2755
19–49	1940	2550
50–59	1900	2550
60–64	1900	2380
65–74	1900	2330

Carbohydrates These energy-providing substances are present in varying amounts in different foods and are found in three main forms: sugars, starches and non-starch polysaccharides (NSP), usually called fibre.

There are two types of sugars: *intrinsic sugars*, which occur naturally in fruit (fructose) and sweet-tasting vegetables, and *extrinsic sugars*, which include lactose (from milk) and all the non-milk extrinsic sugars (NMEs) – sucrose (table sugar), honey, treacle, molasses and so on. The NMEs, or 'added' sugars, provide only calories, whereas foods containing intrinsic sugars also offer vitamins, minerals and fibre. Added sugars (*simple carbohydrates*) are digested and absorbed rapidly to provide energy very quickly. Starches and fibre (*complex carbohydrates*), on the other hand, break down more slowly to offer a longer-term energy source (see also Glycaemic Index). Starchy carbohydrates are found in bread, pasta, rice, wholegrain and breakfast cereals, and potatoes and other starchy vegetables such as parsnips, sweet potatoes and yams.

Healthy eating guidelines recommend that at least half of our daily energy (calories) should come from carbohydrates, and that most of this should be from complex carbohydrates. No more than 11% of our total calorie intake should come from 'added' sugars. For an average woman aged 19–49 years, this would mean a total carbohydrate intake of 259 g per day, of which 202 g should be from starch and intrinsic sugars and no more than 57 g from added sugars. For a man of the same age, total carbohydrates each day should be about 340 g (265 g from starch and intrinsic sugars and 75 g from added sugars).

See also Fibre and Glycogen.

Cholesterol There are two types of cholesterol – the soft waxy substance called blood cholesterol, which is an integral part of human cell membranes, and dietary cholesterol, which is contained in food. *Blood cholesterol* is important in the formation of some hormones and it aids digestion. High blood cholesterol levels are known to be an important risk factor for coronary heart disease, but most of the cholesterol in our blood is made by the liver – only about 25% comes from cholesterol in food. So while it would seem that the amount of cholesterol-rich foods in the diet would have a direct effect on blood cholesterol levels, in fact the best way to reduce blood cholesterol is to eat less saturated fat and to increase intake of foods containing soluble fibre.

Fat Although a small amount of fat is essential for good health, most people consume far too much. Healthy eating guidelines recommend that no more than 33% of our daily energy intake (calories) should come from fat. Each gram of fat contains 9 kcal, more than twice as many calories as carbohydrate or protein, so for a woman aged 19–49 years this means a daily maximum of 71 g fat, and for a man in the same age range 93.5 g fat.

Fats can be divided into 3 main groups: saturated, monounsaturated and polyunsaturated, depending on the chemical structure of the fatty acids they contain. *Saturated fatty acids* are found mainly in animal fats such as butter and other dairy products and in fatty meat. A high intake of saturated fat is known to be a risk factor for coronary heart disease and certain types of cancer. Current guidelines are that no more than 10% of our daily calories should come from saturated fats, which is about 21.5 g for an adult woman and 28.5 g for a man.

Where saturated fats tend to be solid at room temperature, the *unsaturated fatty acids* –

monounsaturated and polyunsaturated – tend to be liquid. *Monounsaturated fats* are found predominantly in olive oil, groundnut (peanut) oil, rapeseed oil and avocados. Foods high in *polyunsaturates* include most vegetable oils – the exceptions are palm oil and coconut oil, both of which are saturated.

Both saturated and monounsaturated fatty acids can be made by the body, but certain polyunsaturated fatty acids – known as *essential fatty acids* – must be supplied by food. There are 2 'families' of these essential fatty acids: *omega-6*, derived from linoleic acid, and *omega-3*, from linolenic acid. The main food sources of the omega-6 family are vegetable oils such as olive and sunflower; omega-3 fatty acids are provided by oily fish, nuts, and vegetable oils such as soya and rapeseed.

When vegetable oils are hydrogenated (hardened) to make margarine and reduced-fat spreads, their unsaturated fatty acids can be changed into trans fatty acids, or '*trans fats*'. These artificially produced trans fats are believed to act in the same way as saturated fats within the body – with the same risks to health. Current healthy eating guidelines suggest that no more than 2% of our daily calories should come from trans fats, which is about 4.3 g for an adult woman and 5.6 g for a man. In thinking about the amount of trans fats you consume, remember that major sources are processed foods such as biscuits, pies, cakes and crisps.

Fibre Technically non-starch polysaccharides (NSP), fibre is the term commonly used to describe several different compounds, such as pectin, hemicellulose, lignin and gums, which are found in the cell walls of all plants. The body cannot digest fibre, nor does it have much nutritional value, but it plays an important role in helping us to stay healthy.

Fibre can be divided into 2 groups – soluble and insoluble. Both types are provided by most plant foods, but some foods are particularly good sources of one type or the other. *Soluble fibre* (in oats, pulses, fruit and vegetables) can help to reduce high blood cholesterol levels and to control blood sugar levels by slowing down the absorption of sugar. *Insoluble fibre* (in wholegrain cereals, pulses, fruit and vegetables) increases stool bulk and speeds the passage of waste material through the body. In this way it helps to prevent constipation, haemorrhoids and diverticular disease, and may protect against bowel cancer.

Our current intake of fibre is around 12 g a day. Healthy eating guidelines suggest that we need to increase this amount to 18 g a day.

Free radicals These highly reactive molecules can cause damage to cell walls and DNA (the genetic material found within cells). They are believed to be involved in the development of heart disease, some cancers and premature ageing. Free radicals are produced naturally by the body in the course of everyday life, but certain factors, such as cigarette smoke, pollution and over-exposure to sunlight, can accelerate their production.

Gluten A protein found in wheat and, to a lesser degree, in rye, barley and oats, but not in corn (maize) or rice. People with *coeliac disease* have a sensitivity to gluten and need to eliminate all gluten-containing foods, such as bread, pasta, cakes and biscuits, from their diet.

Glycaemic Index (GI) This is used to measure the rate at which carbohydrate foods are digested and converted into sugar (glucose) to raise blood sugar levels and provide energy. Foods with a high GI are quickly broken down and offer an immediate energy fix, while those with a lower GI are absorbed more slowly, making you feel full for longer and helping to keep blood sugar levels constant. High-GI foods include table sugar, honey, mashed potatoes and watermelon. Low-GI foods include pulses, wholewheat cereals, apples, cherries, dried apricots, pasta and oats.

Glycogen This is one of the 2 forms in which energy from carbohydrates is made available for use by the body (the other is *glucose*). Whereas glucose is converted quickly from carbohydrates and made available in the blood for a fast energy fix, glycogen is stored in the liver and muscles to fuel longer-term energy needs. When the body has used up its immediate supply of glucose, the stored glycogen is broken down into glucose to continue supplying energy.

Minerals These inorganic substances perform a wide range of vital functions in the body. The *macrominerals* – calcium, chloride, magnesium, potassium, phosphorus and sodium – are needed in relatively large quantities, whereas much smaller amounts are required of the remainder, called *microminerals*. Some microminerals (selenium, magnesium and iodine, for example) are needed in such tiny amounts that they are known as *'trace elements'*.

There are important differences in the body's ability to absorb minerals from different foods, and this can be affected by the presence of other substances. For example, oxalic acid, present in spinach, interferes with the absorption of much of the iron and calcium spinach contains.
• *Calcium* is essential for the development of strong bones and teeth. It also plays an important role in blood clotting. Good sources include dairy products, canned fish (eaten with their bones) and dark green, leafy vegetables.
• *Chloride* helps to maintain the body's fluid balance. The main source in the diet is table salt.
• *Chromium* is important in the regulation of blood sugar levels, as well as levels of fat and cholesterol in the blood. Good dietary sources include red meat, liver, eggs, seafood, cheese and wholegrain cereals.

• *Copper*, component of many enzymes, is needed for bone growth and the formation of connective tissue. It helps the body to absorb iron from food. Good sources include offal, shellfish, mushrooms, cocoa, nuts and seeds.
• *Iodine* is an important component of the thyroid hormones, which govern the rate and efficiency at which food is converted into energy. Good sources include seafood, seaweed and vegetables (depending on the iodine content of the soil in which they are grown).
• *Iron* is an essential component of haemoglobin, the pigment in red blood cells that carries oxygen around the body. Good sources are offal, red meat, dried apricots and prunes, and iron-fortified breakfast cereals.
• *Magnesium* is important for healthy bones, the release of energy from food, and nerve and muscle function. Good sources include wholegrain cereals, peas and other green vegetables, pulses, dried fruit and nuts.
• *Manganese* is a vital component of several enzymes that are involved in energy production and many other functions. Good dietary sources include nuts, cereals, brown rice, pulses and wholemeal bread.
• *Molybdenum* is an essential component of several enzymes, including those involved in the production of DNA. Good sources are offal, yeast, pulses, wholegrain cereals and green leafy vegetables.
• *Phosphorus* is important for healthy bones and teeth and for the release of energy from foods. It is found in most foods. Particularly good sources include dairy products, red meat, poultry, fish and eggs.
• *Potassium*, along with sodium, is important in maintaining fluid balance and regulating blood pressure, and is essential for the transmission of nerve impulses. Good sources include fruit, especially bananas and citrus fruits, nuts, seeds, potatoes and pulses.
• *Selenium* is a powerful antioxidant that protects cells against damage by free radicals. Good dietary sources are meat, fish, dairy foods, brazil nuts, avocados and lentils.
• *Sodium* works with potassium to regulate fluid balance, and is essential for nerve and muscle function. Only a little sodium is needed – we tend to get too much in our diet. The main source in the diet is table salt, as well as salty processed foods and ready-prepared foods.
• *Sulphur* is a component of 2 essential amino acids. Protein foods are the main source.
• *Zinc* is vital for normal growth, as well as reproduction and immunity. Good dietary sources include oysters, red meat, peanuts and sunflower seeds.

Phytochemicals These biologically active compounds, found in most plant foods, are believed to be beneficial in disease prevention. There are literally thousands of different phytochemicals, amongst which are the following:

• *Allicin*, a phytochemical found in garlic, onions, leeks, chives and shallots, is believed to help lower high blood cholesterol levels and stimulate the immune system.
• *Bioflavonoids*, of which there are at least 6000, are found mainly in fruit and sweet-tasting vegetables. Different bioflavonoids have different roles – some are antioxidants, while others act as anti-disease agents. A sub-group of these phytochemicals, called *flavonols*, includes the antioxidant *quercetin*, which is believed to reduce the risk of heart disease and help to protect against cataracts. Quercetin is found in tea, red wine, grapes and broad beans.
• *Carotenoids*, the best known of which are *beta-carotene* and *lycopene*, are powerful antioxidants thought to help protect us against certain types of cancer. Highly coloured fruits and vegetables, such as blackcurrants, mangoes, tomatoes, carrots, sweet potatoes, pumpkin and dark green, leafy vegetables, are excellent sources of carotenoids.
• *Coumarins* are believed to help protect against cancer by inhibiting the formation of tumours. Oranges are a rich source.
• *Glucosinolates*, found mainly in cruciferous vegetables, particularly broccoli, Brussels sprouts, cabbage, kale and cauliflower, are believed to have strong anti-cancer effects. *Sulphoraphane* is one of the powerful cancer-fighting substances produced by glucosinolates.
• *Phytoestrogens* have a chemical structure similar to the female hormone oestrogen, and they are believed to help protect against hormone-related cancers such as breast and prostate cancer. One of the types of these phytochemicals, called *isoflavones*, may also help to relieve symptoms associated with the menopause. Soya beans and chickpeas are a particularly rich source of isoflavones.

Protein This nutrient, necessary for growth and development, for maintenance and repair of cells, and for the production of enzymes, antibodies and hormones, is essential to keep the body working efficiently. Protein is made up of *amino acids*, which are compounds containing the 4 elements that are necessary for life: carbon, hydrogen, oxygen and nitrogen. We need all of the 20 amino acids commonly found in plant and animal proteins. The human body can make 12 of these, but the remaining 8 – called *essential amino acids* – must be obtained from the food we eat.

Protein comes in a wide variety of foods. Meat, fish, dairy products, eggs and soya beans contain all of the essential amino acids, and are therefore called first-class protein foods. Pulses, nuts, seeds and cereals are also good sources of protein, but do not contain the full range of essential amino acids. In practical terms, this really doesn't matter – as long as you include a variety of different protein foods in your diet, your body will get all the amino acids it needs. It is important, though, to eat protein foods every day because the essential amino acids cannot be stored in the body for later use.

The RNI of protein for women aged 19–49 years is 45 g per day and for men of the same age 55 g. In the UK most people eat more protein than they need, although this isn't normally a problem.

Reference Nutrient Intake (RNI) This denotes the average daily amount of vitamins and minerals thought to be sufficient to meet the nutritional needs of almost all individuals within the population. The figures, published by the Department of Health, vary depending on age, sex and specific nutritional needs such as pregnancy. RNIs are equivalent to what used to be called Recommended Daily Amounts or Allowances (RDA).

RNIs for adults (19–49 years)

Vitamin A	600–700 mcg
Vitamin B_1	0.8 mg for women, 1 mg for men
Vitamin B_2	1.1 mg for women, 1.3 mg for men
Niacin	13 mg for women, 17 mg for men
Vitamin B_6	1.2 mg for women, 1.4 mg for men
Vitamin B_{12}	1.5 mg
Folate	200 mcg (400 mcg for first trimester of pregnancy)
Vitamin C	40 mg
Vitamin E	no recommendation in the UK; the EC RDA is 10 mg, which has been used in all recipe analyses in this book
Calcium	700 mg
Chloride	2500 mg
Copper	1.2 mg
Iodine	140 mcg
Iron	14.8 mg for women, 8.7 mg for men
Magnesium	270–300 mg
Phosphorus	550 mg
Potassium	3500 mg
Selenium	60 mcg for women, 75 mcg for men
Sodium	1600 mg
Zinc	7 mg for women, 9.5 mg for men

Vitamins These are organic compounds that are essential for good health. Although they are required in only small amounts, each one has specific vital functions to perform. Most vitamins cannot be made by the human body, and therefore must be obtained from the diet. The body is capable of storing some vitamins (A, D, E, K and B_{12}), but the rest need to be provided by the diet on a regular basis. A well-balanced diet, containing a wide variety of different foods, is the best way to ensure that you get all the vitamins you need.

Vitamins can be divided into 2 groups: *water-soluble* (B complex and C) and *fat-soluble* (A, D, E and K). Water-soluble vitamins are easily destroyed during processing, storage, and the preparation and cooking of food. The fat-soluble vitamins are less vulnerable to losses during cooking and processing.

• *Vitamin A* (retinol) is essential for healthy vision, eyes, skin and growth. Good sources include dairy products, offal (especially liver), eggs and oily fish. Vitamin A can also be obtained from *beta-carotene*, the pigment found in highly coloured fruit and vegetables. In addition to acting as a source of vitamin A, beta-carotene has an important role to play as an antioxidant in its own right.

• *The B Complex vitamins* have very similar roles to play in nutrition, and many of them occur together in the same foods.
Vitamin B_1 (thiamin) is essential in the release of energy from carbohydrates. Good sources include milk, offal, meat (especially pork), wholegrain and fortified breakfast cereals, nuts and pulses, yeast extract and wheat germ. White flour and bread are fortified with B_1 in the UK.
Vitamin B_2 (riboflavin) is vital for growth, healthy skin and eyes, and the release of energy from food. Good sources include milk, meat, offal, eggs, cheese, fortified breakfast cereals, yeast extract and green leafy vegetables.
Niacin (nicotinic acid), sometimes called vitamin B_3, plays an important role in the release of energy within the cells. Unlike the other B vitamins it can be made by the body from the essential amino acid tryptophan. Good sources include meat, offal, fish, fortified breakfast cereals and pulses. White flour and bread are fortified with niacin in the UK.
Pantothenic acid, sometimes called vitamin B_5, is involved in a number of metabolic reactions, including energy production. This vitamin is present in most foods; notable exceptions are fat, oil and sugar. Good sources include liver, kidneys, yeast, egg yolks, fish roe, wheat germ, nuts, pulses and fresh vegetables.
Vitamin B_6 (pyridoxine) helps the body to utilise protein and contributes to the formation of haemoglobin for red blood cells. B_6 is found in a wide range of foods including meat, liver, fish, eggs, wholegrain cereals, some vegetables, pulses, brown rice, nuts and yeast extract.
Vitamin B_{12} (cyanocobalamin) is vital for growth, the formation of red blood cells and maintenance of a healthy nervous system. B_{12} is unique in that it is principally found in foods of animal origin. Vegetarians who eat dairy products will get enough, but vegans need to ensure they include food fortified with B_{12} in their diet. Good sources of B_{12} include liver, kidneys, oily fish, meat, cheese, eggs and milk.
Folate (folic acid) is involved in the manufacture of amino acids and in the production of red blood cells. Recent research suggests that folate may also help to protect against heart disease. Good sources of folate are green leafy vegetables, liver, pulses, eggs, wholegrain cereal products and fortified breakfast cereals, brewers' yeast, wheatgerm, nuts and fruit, especially grapefruit and oranges.
Biotin is needed for various metabolic reactions and the release of energy from foods. Good sources include liver, oily fish, brewers' yeast, kidneys, egg yolks and brown rice.

• *Vitamin C* (ascorbic acid) is essential for growth and vital for the formation of collagen (a protein needed for healthy bones, teeth, gums, blood capillaries and all connective tissue). It plays an important role in the healing of wounds and fractures, and acts as a powerful antioxidant. Vitamin C is found mainly in fruit and vegetables.

• *Vitamin D* (cholecalciferol) is essential for growth and the absorption of calcium, and thus for the formation of healthy bones. It is also involved in maintaining a healthy nervous system. The amount of vitamin D occurring naturally in foods is small, and it is found in very few foods – good sources are oily fish (and fish liver oil supplements), eggs and liver, as well as breakfast cereals, margarine and full-fat milk that are fortified with vitamin D. Most vitamin D, however, does not come from the diet but is made by the body when the skin is exposed to sunlight.

• *Vitamin E* is not one vitamin, but a number of related compounds called tocopherols that function as antioxidants. Good sources of vitamin E are vegetable oils, polyunsaturated margarines, wheatgerm, sunflower seeds, nuts, oily fish, eggs, wholegrain cereals, avocados and spinach.

• *Vitamin K* is essential for the production of several proteins, including prothombin which is involved in the clotting of blood. It has been found to exist in 3 forms, one of which is obtained from food while the other 2 are made by the bacteria in the intestine. Vitamin K_1, which is the form found in food, is present in broccoli, cabbage, spinach, milk, margarine, vegetable oils, particularly soya oil, cereals, liver, alfalfa and kelp.

Nutritional analyses

The nutritional analysis of each recipe has been carried out using data from *The Composition of Foods* with additional data from food manufacturers where appropriate. Because the level and availability of different nutrients can vary, depending on factors like growing conditions and breed of animal, the figures are intended as an approximate guide only.

The analyses include vitamins A, B_1, B_2, B_6, B_{12}, niacin, folate, C, D and E, and the minerals calcium, copper, iron, potassium, selenium and zinc. Other vitamins and minerals are not included, as deficiencies are rare. Optional ingredients and optional serving suggestions have not been included in the calculations.

Index

index

Printing and binding:
Printer Industria
   Gráfica S.A.,Barcelona
Separations: Litho Origination,
London
Paper: Condat, France

index

616-011-1